THE LOVE OF THE NIGHTINGALE

AND

THE GRACE OF MARY TRAVERSE

THE LOVE OF
THE NIGHTINGALE

AND

THE GRACE OF
MARY TRAVERSE

TIMBERLAKE
WERTENBAKER

faber and faber
LONDON · BOSTON

First published in 1989
by Faber and Faber Limited
3 Queen Square London WCIN 3AU

An earlier version of *The Grace of Mary Traverse*
was first published in a single volume in 1985

Photoset by Wilmaset Birkenhead Wirral
Printed in England by
Clays Ltd, St Ives plc

All rights in these plays are strictly reserved and
applications for performances should be made in advance,
before rehearsals begin, to Michael Imison Playwrights Limited,
28 Almeida Street, London NI

A CIP record for this book is available from the British Library

ISBN 0–571–15383–6

2 4 6 8 10 9 7 5 3

CONTENTS

THE LOVE OF THE NIGHTINGALE

For Kate

Listen. This is the noise of myth. It makes
the same sound as shadow. Can you hear it?

Eavan Boland, 'The Journey'

Now, by myself, I am nothing; yea, full oft
I have regarded woman's fortunes thus,
That we are nothing; who in our fathers' house
Live, I suppose, the happiest, while young,
Of all mankind; for ever pleasantly
Does Folly nurture all. Then, when we come
To full discretion and maturity,
We are thrust out and marketed abroad,
Far from our parents and ancestral gods,
Some to strange husbands, some to barbarous,
One to a rude, one to a wrangling home;
And these, after the yoking of a night,
We are bound to like, and deem it well with us.

Much
I envy thee thy life: and most of all,
That thou hast never had experience
Of a strange land.

Two fragments from Sophocles's lost play, *Tereus*
Translated by Sir George Young

The Love of the Nightingale was first performed by the Royal Shakespeare Company at The Other Place, Stratford-upon-Avon, on 28 October 1988. The cast was as follows:

MALE CHORUS	David Acton, Stephen Gordon, Richard Haddon Haines, Patrick Miller, Edward Rawle-Hicks
FIRST SOLDIER	Patrick Miller
SECOND SOLDIER	David Acton
PROCNE	Marie Mullen
PHILOMELE	Katy Behean
KING PANDION	Richard Haddon Haines
THE QUEEN	Joan Blackham
TEREUS	Peter Lennon

Female Chorus

HERO	Cate Hamer
IRIS	Claudette Williams
JUNE	Joan Blackham
ECHO	Joanna Roth
HELEN	Jill Spurrier

Actors in the Hippolytus play

APHRODITE	Claudette Williams
PHAEDRA	Cate Hamer
THE NURSE	Jill Spurrier
FEMALE CHORUS	Joanna Roth
HIPPOLYTUS	Edward Rawle-Hicks
THESEUS	David Acton
MALE CHORUS	Stephen Gordon
THE CAPTAIN	Tony Armatrading
NIOBE	Jenni George

SERVANT	Joanna Roth
ITYS	Nicholas Besley/Alexander Knott
Director	Garry Hynes
Lighting	Geraint Pughe
Music	Ilona Sekacz

NOTE ON THE CHORUS
The Chorus never speak together, except the one time it is
specifically indicated in the text.

Athens. The MALE CHORUS.

MALE CHORUS: War.
  (*Two* SOLDIERS *come on, with swords and shields.*)
FIRST SOLDIER: You cur!
SECOND SOLDIER: You cat's whisker.
FIRST SOLDIER: You flea's foot.
SECOND SOLDIER: You particle.
  (*Pause.*)
  You son of a bitch.
FIRST SOLDIER: You son of a lame hyena.
SECOND SOLDIER: You son of a bleeding whore.
FIRST SOLDIER: You son of a woman!
  (*Pause.*)
  I'll slice your drooping genitalia.
SECOND SOLDIER: I'll pierce your windy asshole.
FIRST SOLDIER: I'll drink from your skull.
  (*Pause.*)
  Coward!
SECOND SOLDIER: Braggard.
FIRST SOLDIER: You worm.
SECOND SOLDIER: You – man.
  (*They fight.*)
MALE CHORUS: And now, death.
  (*The* FIRST SOLDIER *kills the* SECOND SOLDIER.)
SECOND SOLDIER: Murderer!
FIRST SOLDIER: Corpse!
MALE CHORUS: We begin here because no life ever has been
  untouched by war.
MALE CHORUS: Everyone loves to discuss war.
MALE CHORUS: And yet its outcome, death, is shrouded in
  silence.

I

MALE CHORUS: Wars make death acceptable. The gods are less cruel if it is man's fault.

MALE CHORUS: Perhaps, but this is not our story. War is the inevitable background, the ruins in the distance establishing place and perspective.

MALE CHORUS: Athens is at war, but in the palace of the Athenian king Pandion, two sisters discuss life's charms and the attractions of men.

SCENE 2

PROCNE, PHILOMELE.

PROCNE: Don't say that, Philomele.

PHILOMELE: It's the truth: he's so handsome I want to wrap my legs around him.

PROCNE: That's not how it's done.

PHILOMELE: How can I know if no one will tell me? Look at the sweat shining down his body. My feet will curl around the muscles of his back. How is it done, Procne, tell me, please? If you don't tell me, I'll ask Niobe and she'll tell me all wrong.

PROCNE: I'll tell you if you tell me something.

PHILOMELE: I'll tell you everything I know, sweet sister. (*Pause.*) I don't know anything.

PROCNE: You know yourself.

PHILOMELE: Oh, yes, I feel such things, Procne, such things. Tigers, rivers, serpents, here, in my stomach, a little below. I'll tell you how the serpent uncurls inside me if you tell me how it's done.

PROCNE: That's not what I meant. Philomele, I'm going to marry soon.

PHILOMELE: I envy you, sister, you'll know everything then. What are they like? Men?

PROCNE: Look: they fight.

PHILOMELE: What are they like: naked?

PROCNE: Spongy.

PHILOMELE: What?

PROCNE: I haven't seen one yet, but that's what they told me to prepare me. They have sponges.

PHILOMELE: Where?

PROCNE: Here. Getting bigger and smaller and moving up and down. I didn't listen very carefully, I'll know soon enough. Philomele, when I am married, will you want to come and visit me?

PHILOMELE: Yes, sister, yes. I'll visit you every day and you'll let me watch.

PROCNE: Philomele! Can't you think of anything else?

PHILOMELE: Not today. Tomorrow I'll think about wisdom. It must be so beautiful. Warm ripples of light.

PROCNE: I think most of it you can do on your own. The sponge. I think it detaches.

PHILOMELE: I wouldn't want to do it on my own. I want to run my hands down bronzed skin. Ah, I can feel the tiger again.

PROCNE: If I went far away, would you still want to come and visit me?

PHILOMELE: I will cross any sea to visit you and your handsome husband, sister. (*Pause.*) When I'm old enough, I won't stop doing it, whatever it is. Life must be so beautiful when you're older. It's beautiful now. Sometimes I'm so happy.

PROCNE: Quiet, Philomele! Never say you're happy. It wakes up the gods and then they look at you and that is never a good thing. Take it back, now.

PHILOMELE: You taught me not to lie, sister.

PROCNE: I wish I didn't have to leave home. I worry about you.

PHILOMELE: Life is sweet, my sister, and I love everything in it. The feelings. Athens. You. And that brave young warrior fighting to protect us. Oh!

PROCNE: Philomele? Ah.
He's dead.

PHILOMELE: Crumpled. Procne, was it my fault? Should I have held my tongue?

PROCNE: Athens is at war, men must die.

PHILOMELE: I'm frightened. I don't want to leave this room, ever.

PROCNE: You must try to become more moderate. Measure in all things, remember, it's what the philosophers recommend.

PHILOMELE: Will the philosophers start speaking again after the war? Procne, can we go and listen to them?

PROCNE: I won't be here.

PHILOMELE: Procne, don't go.

PROCNE: It's our parents' will. They know best.
  (*Pause.*)
  You will come to me if I ask for you, you will?

PHILOMELE: Yes.

PROCNE: I want you to promise. Remember you must never break a promise.

PHILOMELE: I promise. I will want to. I promise again.

PROCNE: That makes me happy. Ah.

SCENE 3

The palace of King Pandion. KING PANDION, *the* QUEEN, TEREUS, PROCNE, PHILOMELE, *the* MALE CHORUS.

MALE CHORUS: Athens won the war with the help of an ally from the north.

MALE CHORUS: The leader of the liberators was called Tereus.

KING PANDION: No liberated country is ungrateful. That is a rule. You will take what you want from our country. It will be given with gratitude. We are ready.

TEREUS: I came not out of greed but in the cause of justice, King Pandion. But I have come to love this country and its inhabitants.

4

QUEEN: (*To* KING PANDION) He wants to stay! I knew it!
(*Pause.*)

KING PANDION: Of course if you wish to stay in Athens that is your right. We can only remind you this is a small city. But you must stay if you wish.

TEREUS: No. I must go back north. There has been trouble while I've conducted this war. What I want – is to bring some of your country to mine, its manners, its ease, its civilized discourse.

QUEEN: (*To* KING PANDION) I knew it: he wants Procne.

KING PANDION: I can send you some of our tutors. The philosophers, I'm afraid, are rather independent.

TEREUS: I have always believed that culture was kept by the women.

KING PANDION: Ours are not encouraged to go abroad.

TEREUS: But they have a reputation for wisdom. Is that false?

QUEEN: Be careful, he's crafty.

KING PANDION: It is true. Our women are the best.

TEREUS: So.

QUEEN: I knew it.
(*Pause.*)

KING PANDION: She's yours, Tereus. Procne –

PROCNE: But, Father –

KING PANDION: Your husband.

PROCNE: Mother –

QUEEN: What can I say?

KING PANDION: I am only sad you will live so far away.

PHILOMELE: Can I go with her?

QUEEN: Quiet, child.

TEREUS: (*To* PROCNE) I will love and respect you.

MALE CHORUS: It didn't happen that quickly. It took months and much indirect discourse. But that is the gist of it. The end was known from the beginning.

MALE CHORUS: After an elaborate wedding in which King Pandion solemnly gave his daughter to the hero, Tereus, the two left for Thrace. There was relief in Athens. His army had become expensive, rude, rowdy.

MALE CHORUS: Had always been, but we see things differently in peace. That is why peace is so painful.

MALE CHORUS: Nothing to blur the waters. We look down to the bottom.

MALE CHORUS: And on a clear day, we see our own reflections. (*Pause.*)

MALE CHORUS: In due course, Procne had a child, a boy called Itys. Five years passed.

SCENE 4

PROCNE *and her companions, the* FEMALE CHORUS: HERO, ECHO, IRIS, JUNE, HELEN.

PROCNE: Where have all the words gone?

HERO: She sits alone, hour after hour, turns her head away and laments.

IRIS: We don't know how to act, we don't know what to say.

HERO: She turns from us in grief.

JUNE: Boredom.

ECHO: Homesick.

HERO: It is difficult to come to a strange land.

HELEN: You will always be a guest there, never call it your own, never rest in the kindness of history.

ECHO: Your story intermingled with events, no. You will be outside.

IRIS: And if it is the land of your husband can you even say you have chosen it?

JUNE: She is not one of us.

HERO: A shared childhood makes friends between women.

ECHO: The places we walked together, our first smells.

HELEN: But an unhappy woman can do much harm. She has already dampened our play.

JUNE: Mocked the occupation of our hours, scorned.

IRIS: What shall we do?

HELEN: I fear the future.

6

PROCNE: Where have the words gone?

ECHO: Gone, Procne, the words?

PROCNE: There were so many. Everything that was had a word
and every word was something. None of these meanings
half in the shade, unclear.

IRIS: We speak the same language, Procne.

PROCNE: The words are the same, but point to different things.
We aspire to clarity in sound, you like the silences in
between.

HERO: We offered to initiate you.

PROCNE: Barbarian practices. I am an Athenian: I know the
truth is found by logic and happiness lies in the truth.

HERO: Truth is full of darkness.

PROCNE: No, truth is good and beautiful. See . . . (*Pause.*) I
must have someone to talk to.

JUNE: We've tried. See . . .

HERO: She turns away.

PROCNE: How we talked. Our words played, caressed each
other, our words were tossed lightly, a challenge to catch.
Where is she now? Who shares those games with her? Or is
she silent too?

ECHO: Silent, Procne, who?

PROCNE: My sister. (*Pause.*) My friend. I want to talk to her. I
want her here.

HERO: You have a family, Procne, a husband, a child.

PROCNE: I cannot talk to my husband. I have nothing to say to
my son. I want her here. She must come here.

HELEN: It's a long way and a dangerous one for a young girl.

HELEN: Let her be, Procne.

PROCNE: I want my sister here.

HELEN: She could come to harm.

PROCNE: Tereus could bring her, she'll be safe with him.

ECHO: Tereus.

HELEN: Dangers on the sea, he won't want you to risk them.

PROCNE: He can go alone. I'll wait here and look after the
country.

ECHO: Tereus.

HERO: Will your sister want to come to a strange land?
PROCNE: She will want what I want.
HELEN: Don't ask her to come, Procne.
PROCNE: Why not?
HERO: This is no country for a strange young girl.
PROCNE: She will be with me.
HERO: She won't listen.
HELEN: I am worried. It is not something I can say. There are
no words for forebodings.
HERO: We are only brushed by possibilities.
ECHO: A beating of wings.
JUNE: Best to say nothing. Procne? May we go now?
PROCNE: To your rituals?
JUNE: Yes, it's time.
PROCNE: Very well, go.
   (*They go.*)
   This silence . . . this silence . . .

SCENE 5

The theatre in Athens. KING PANDION, TEREUS, HIPPOLYTUS,
THESEUS.

KING PANDION: Procne has always been so sensible. Why,
suddenly, does she ask for her sister?
TEREUS: She didn't explain. She insisted I come to you and I
did what she asked.
KING PANDION: I understand, Tereus, but such a long
journey . . . Procne's not ill?
TEREUS: She was well when I left. She has her child,
companions.
KING PANDION: Philomele is still very young. And yet, I
allowed Procne to go so far away . . . What do you think,
Tereus?
TEREUS: You're her father.
KING PANDION: And you, her husband.

8

TEREUS: I only meant Procne would accept any decision you made. It is a long journey.

(APHRODITE *enters*.)

APHRODITE: I am Aphrodite, goddess of love, resplendent and mighty, revered on earth, courted in heaven, all pay tribute to my fearful power.

KING PANDION: Do you know this play, Tereus?

TEREUS: No.

KING PANDION: I find plays help me think. You catch a phrase, recognize a character. Perhaps this play will help us come to a decision.

APHRODITE: I honour those who kneel before me, but that proud heart which dares defy me, that haughty heart I bring low.

TEREUS: That's sound.

KING PANDION: Do you have good theatre in Thrace?

TEREUS: We prefer sport.

KING PANDION: Then you are like Hippolytus.

TEREUS: Who?

KING PANDION: Listen.

APHRODITE: Hippolytus turns his head away. Hippolytus prefers the hard chase to the soft bed, wild game to foreplay, but chaste Hippolytus shall be crushed this very day.

(APHRODITE *exits. The* QUEEN *and* PHILOMELE *enter*.)

PHILOMELE: We're late! I've missed Aphrodite.

KING PANDION: She only told us it was going to end badly, but we already know that. It's a tragedy.

(*Enter* PHAEDRA.)

QUEEN: There's Phaedra. (*To* TEREUS.) Phaedra is married to Theseus, the King of Athens. Hippolytus is Theseus' son by his previous mistress, the Amazon Queen, who's now dead, and so Phaedra's stepson. Phaedra has three children of her own.

PHAEDRA: Hold me, hold me, hold up my head. The strength of my limbs is melting away.

9

PHILOMELE: How beautiful to love like that! The strength of my limbs is melting away. Is that what you feel for Procne, Tereus?

QUEEN: Philomele! (*To* TEREUS) Phaedra's fallen in love with Hippolytus.

TEREUS: Her own stepson! That's wrong.

KING PANDION: That's what makes it a tragedy. When you love the right person it's a comedy.

PHAEDRA: Oh, pity me, pity me, what have I done? What will become of me? I have strayed from the path of good sense.

TEREUS: Why should we pity her? These plays condone vice.

KING PANDION: Perhaps they only show us the uncomfortable folds of the human heart.

PHAEDRA: I am mad, struck down by the malice of the implacable god.

PHILOMELE: You see, Tereus, love is a god and you cannot control him.

QUEEN: Here's the nurse. She always gives advice.
(*The* NURSE *enters.*)

NURSE: So: you love. You are not the first nor the last. You want to kill yourself? Must all who love die? No, Phaedra, the god has stricken you, how dare you rebel? Be bold, and love. That is god's will.

TEREUS: Terrible advice.

PHILOMELE: No, Tereus, you must obey the gods. Are you blasphemous up there in Thrace?

KING PANDION: Philomele, you are talking to a king.

TEREUS: And to a brother, let her speak, Pandion.

NURSE: I have a remedy. Trust me.

KING PANDION: Procne has asked for you. She wants you to go back with Tereus to Thrace.

PHILOMELE: To Thrace? To Procne? Oh, yes.

KING PANDION: You want to leave your parents? Athens?

PHILOMELE: I promised Procne I would go if she ever asked for me.

KING PANDION: You were a child.

TEREUS: We have no theatre or even philosophers in Thrace, Philomele.

PHILOMELE: I have to keep my word.

TEREUS: Why?

PHILOMELE: Because that is honourable, Tereus.

QUEEN: Listen to the chorus. The playwright always speaks through the chorus.

FEMALE CHORUS: Love, stealing with grace into the heart you wish to destroy, love, turning us blind with the bitter poison of desire, love, come not my way. And when you whirl through the streets, wild steps to unchained rhythms, love, I pray you, brush not against me, love, I beg you, pass me by.

TEREUS: Ah!

PHILOMELE: I would never say that, would you, brother Tereus? I want to feel everything there is to feel. Don't you?

TEREUS: No!

KING PANDION: Tereus, what's the matter?

TEREUS: Nothing. The heat.

PHAEDRA: Oh, I am destroyed for ever.

PHILOMELE: Poor Phaedra.

TEREUS: You pity her, Philomele?

QUEEN: Hippolytus has just heard in what way Phaedra loves him. He's furious.

HIPPOLYTUS: Woman, counterfeit coin, why did the gods put you in the world? If we must have sons, let us buy them in the temples and bypass the concourse of these noxious women. I hate you women, hate, hate and hate you.

PHILOMELE: This is horrible. It's not Phaedra's fault she loves him.

TEREUS: She could keep silent about it.

PHILOMELE: When you love you want to imprison the one you love in your words, in your tenderness.

TEREUS: How do you know all this, Philomele?

PHILOMELE: Sometimes I feel the whole world beating inside me.

TEREUS: Philomele . . .

(PHAEDRA *screams offstage, then staggers on.*)

QUEEN: Phaedra's killed herself and there's Theseus just back from his travels.

THESEUS: My wife! What have I said or done to drive you to this horrible death? She calls me to her, she can still speak. What prayers, what orders, what entreaties do you leave your grieving husband? Oh, my poor love, speak! (*He listens.*) Hippolytus! Has dared to rape my wife!

TEREUS: Phaedra has lied! That's vile.

PHILOMELE: Why destroy what you love? It's the god.

THESEUS: Father Poseidon, great and ancient sea-god, you once allotted me three wishes. With one of these, I pray you now, kill my son.

QUEEN: That happens offstage. A giant wave comes out of the sea and crashes Hippolytus's chariot against the rocks. Here's the male chorus.

MALE CHORUS: Sometimes I believe in a kind power, wise and all-knowing but when I see the acts of men and their destinies, my hopes grow dim. Fortune twists and turns and life is endless wandering.

KING PANDION: The play's coming to an end, and I still haven't reached a decision. Queen . . .

MALE CHORUS: What I want from life is to be ordinary.

PHILOMELE: How boring.

QUEEN: Hippolytus has come back to Athens to die. He's wounded. The head.

FEMALE CHORUS: Poor Hippolytus, I weep at your pitiful fate. And I rage against the gods who sent you far away, out of your father's lands to meet with such disaster from the sea-god's wave.

KING PANDION: That's the phrase. Philomele, you must not leave your father's lands. You'll stay here.

PHILOMELE: But, Father, I'm not Hippolytus. You haven't cursed me. And Tereus isn't Phaedra, look.

(*She laughs.*)

TEREUS: I have expert sailors, I don't think we'll crash against the rocks.

KING PANDION: It's such a long journey.

TEREUS: We'll travel swiftly. Procne is so impatient to see her sister. We must go soon, or she'll fall ill with worry.

KING PANDION: When?

TEREUS: Tomorrow.

HIPPOLYTUS: Weep for me, weep for me, destroyed, mangled, trampled underfoot by man and god both unjust, weep, weep for my death.

PHILOMELE: Ah.

TEREUS: You're crying, Philomele.

PHILOMELE: I felt, I felt – the beating of wings . . .

KING PANDION: You do not have to go.

PHILOMELE: It's the play, I am so sorry for them all. I have to go. My promise . . .

KING PANDION: (To QUEEN) It's only a visit, Philomele will come back to us.

QUEEN: Where is she going?

KING PANDION: To Thrace! Weren't you listening?

MALE AND FEMALE CHORUS: (Together) These sorrows have fallen upon us unforeseen.

MALE CHORUS: Fate is irresistible.

FEMALE CHORUS: And there is no escape.

KING PANDION: And now we must applaud the actors.

SCENE 6

A small ship, sailing north. The MALE CHORUS, PHILOMELE, TEREUS, *the* CAPTAIN.

MALE CHORUS: The journey north:
Row gently out of Piraeus on a starlit night. Sail around Cape Sounion with a good wind, over to Kea for water and provisions. Kea to Andros, a quiet sea. Up the coast of Euboea to the Sporades: Skiathos, Paparethos, Gioura,

Pathoura. Skirt the three fingered promontory of the main-
land: Kassandra, Sithounia and Athos of the wild men and
into the Thracian sea. The dawns, so loved by the poets.

MALE CHORUS: Rosy fingered, female.

MALE CHORUS: The dawns get colder and colder as we sail
north.

(*Pause*.)

MALE CHORUS: Philomele wonders at the beauty of the sea.

MALE CHORUS: Tereus wonders at Philomele's beauty.

MALE CHORUS: We say nothing. And when the order comes.

MALE CHORUS: Such an order.

MALE CHORUS: Six Athenian soldiers have been sent to
accompany Philomele. They stand on the deck, watching.
On a dark night, they disappear.

(*Pause*.)

MALE CHORUS: In the cold dawns, Tereus burns.

MALE CHORUS: Does Philomele know? Ought we to tell her?
We are here only to observe, journalists of an antique
world, putting horror into words, unable to stop the events
we will soon record.

MALE CHORUS: And so we reach the lonely port of Imeros. It is
dark, there is no welcome.

MALE CHORUS: We are not expected.

MALE CHORUS: No moon in the sky.

MALE CHORUS: This is unpropitious.

MALE CHORUS: But that we already knew. Could we have done
something? And now?

MALE CHORUS: We choose to be accurate, and we record:

SCENE 7

The CAPTAIN, PHILOMELE, NIOBE.

PHILOMELE: Where are we now, Captain?

CAPTAIN: Far north of Athens, miss.

PHILOMELE: I know that, Captain. How far are we from
Thrace?

14

CAPTAIN: A few days, perhaps more. It depends.

PHILOMELE: On you?

CAPTAIN: No. On the sea.

PHILOMELE: Isn't that a fire over there?

CAPTAIN: Yes.

PHILOMELE: That means we're not far from the coast, doesn't it?

CAPTAIN: Yes, it does.

PHILOMELE: Look how high the fire is. It must be a mountain, Captain.

CAPTAIN: Yes, it is.

PHILOMELE: What is it called, Captain, what is it like? I would like to know about all these lands. You must tell me.

CAPTAIN: That would be Mount Athos, miss.

PHILOMELE: Why don't we anchor there, Captain, and climb the mountain?

CAPTAIN: You wouldn't want to go there, miss.

PHILOMELE: Why not, is it ugly?

CAPTAIN: No, but wild men live there, very wild. They kill all women, even female animals are not allowed on that mountain.

PHILOMELE: Why not?

CAPTAIN: They worship male gods. They believe all harm in the world comes from women.

PHILOMELE: Why do they believe that? (*Pause.*) You don't agree with them, do you, Captain?

CAPTAIN: I don't know, miss.

PHILOMELE: If you don't disagree, you agree with them, Captain, that's logic.

CAPTAIN: Women are beautiful.

PHILOMELE: But surely you believe that beauty is truth and goodness as well?

CAPTAIN: That I don't know. I would have to think about it.

PHILOMELE: I'll prove it to you now, I once heard a philosopher do it. I will begin by asking you a lot of questions. You answer yes or no. But you must pay attention. Are you ready?

CAPTAIN: I think so.

PHILOMELE: And when I've proved all this, Captain, you will have to renounce the beliefs of those wild men.

CAPTAIN: I might.

PHILOMELE: You have to promise.

(TEREUS *enters*.)

TEREUS: Why are the sails up, Captain?

CAPTAIN: We have a good wind, Tereus.

TEREUS: Take them down.

CAPTAIN: We could be becalmed further north and then my men will have to row. They're tired, Tereus.

TEREUS: We're sailing too fast, it's frightening Philomele.

PHILOMELE: I love to feel the wind, Tereus.

TEREUS: Why aren't you asleep?

PHILOMELE: It's such a beautiful night. I was watching the fires on Athos.

TEREUS: Athos? Yes, the hooded men.

PHILOMELE: The Captain was telling me about them.

TEREUS: Lower the sails, Captain.

CAPTAIN: But Tereus –

TEREUS: This isn't a battle, we have time.

(*Exit the* CAPTAIN.)

NIOBE: I'll take Philomele down with me, my lord.

TEREUS: Not yet.

(*Pause*.)

Come and talk to me, Philomele.

NIOBE: Entertain his lordship, Philomele.

(*Silence*.)

TEREUS: Well. You were talking easily enough when I came above.

PHILOMELE: Tell me about my sister, Tereus.

TEREUS: I've already told you.

PHILOMELE: Tell me more. How does she occupy her time?

TEREUS: I don't know. She has women with her.

PHILOMELE: What do they talk about?

TEREUS: What women talk about. I didn't ask you to grill me, Philomele. Talk to me. Talk to me about the night.

16

PHILOMELE: The night?
(*Pause.*)
TEREUS: The night. Something! What were you saying to the
   captain?
PHILOMELE: I was asking him questions, Tereus.
   (*Silence. The* SAILORS *sing a song, softly.*)
PHILOMELE: How well they sing.
   (*Pause.*)
TEREUS: Do you want to be married, Philomele?
NIOBE: Oh, yes, my lord. Every young girl wants to be
   married. Don't you, Philomele?
PHILOMELE: Niobe, go to bed, please.
NIOBE: No, I can't. I mustn't. I will stay here. I must.
PHILOMELE: Why?
NIOBE: It wouldn't be right . . . A young girl. A man.
PHILOMELE: I am with my brother, Niobe.
TEREUS: You can go, Niobe.
NIOBE: Yes, yes. Well . . . I will go and talk to the sailors.
   Although what they will say to an old woman . . . no one
   wants to talk to an old woman. But so it is . . . I'm not far,
   I'm not far. The Queen said I was not to go far . . .
   (*Pause.*)
TEREUS: You're beautiful.
PHILOMELE: Procne always said I was. But the Athenians
   admired her because of her dignity. Has she kept that in all
   her years?
TEREUS: In the moonlight, your skin seems transparent.
PHILOMELE: We used to put water out in the full moon and
   wash our faces in it. We thought it would give us the skin
   of a goddess. I still do it in memory of my sister. Does she
   still let out that rhythmical laugh when she thinks you're
   being foolish? Always on one note, then stopped abruptly.
   Does she laugh with her women?
TEREUS: I don't know . . .
PHILOMELE: Does she laugh at you?
TEREUS: Philomele.
PHILOMELE: Yes, brother.

TEREUS: What sort of man do you want to marry? A king?

PHILOMELE: Why not? A great king. Or a prince. Or a noble captain.

TEREUS: Not necessarily from Athens?

PHILOMELE: No. As long as he is wise.

TEREUS: Wise?

PHILOMELE: But then, all kings are wise, aren't they? They have to be or they wouldn't be kings.

TEREUS: You are born a king. Nothing can change that.

PHILOMELE: But you still have to deserve it, don't you?

TEREUS: Would you marry a king from the north? Like your sister? Would you do as your sister in all things?

PHILOMELE: What do you mean? Oh, look, they're making fun of Niobe. Niobe! Here!

NIOBE: They say I would be beautiful if I were young and if I were beautiful then I would be young, no one is kind to an old woman, but I don't mind, I've seen the world. You made his lordship laugh, Philomele, I heard it, that's good. All is well when power smiles, that I know.

TEREUS: Philomele wants to marry a king from the north.

NIOBE: Why yes, a man as great and brave as you.

PHILOMELE: I am happy for my sister and that is enough for me.

NIOBE: Sisters, sisters . . .

TEREUS: If Procne were . . .

NIOBE: I had sisters . . .

PHILOMELE: Procne.

TEREUS: To become ill . . .

PHILOMELE: What are you saying, Tereus? Wasn't she well when you left? Why didn't you tell me? Why are we going so slowly? Tell the captain to go faster.

TEREUS: I didn't say that, but if . . .

NIOBE: Yes, I had many sisters.

TEREUS: Things happen.

NIOBE: Too many . . .

PHILOMELE: My love will protect her, and yours too, Tereus.

TEREUS: Yes . . . But should . . .

NIOBE: They died.
PHILOMELE: Niobe!
NIOBE: I only want to help. I know the world. Old women do.
But I'll be quiet now, very quiet.
PHILOMELE: Sister. We will be so happy.
TEREUS: Philomele . . .

SCENE 8

The MALE CHORUS.

MALE CHORUS: What is a myth? The oblique image of an
unwanted truth, reverberating through time.
MALE CHORUS: And yet, the first, the Greek meaning of myth,
is simply what is delivered by word of mouth, a myth is
speech, public speech.
MALE CHORUS: And myth also means the matter itself, the
content of the speech.
MALE CHORUS: We might ask, has the content become
increasingly unacceptable and therefore the speech more
indirect? How has the meaning of myth been transformed
from public speech to an unlikely story? It also meant
counsel, command. Now it is a remote tale.
MAL CHORUS: Let that be, there is no content without its myth.
Fathers and sons, rebellion, collaboration, the state, every
fold and twist of passion, we have uttered them all. This
one, you will say, watching Philomele watching Tereus
watching Philomele, must be about men and women, yes,
you think, a myth for our times, we understand.
MALE CHORUS: You will be beside the myth. If you must think
of anything, think of countries, silence, but we cannot
rephrase it for you. If we could, why would we trouble to
show you the myth?
We row Philomele north. Does she notice the widening
cracks in that fragile edifice, happiness? And what about

Procne, the cause perhaps, in any case the motor of a myth
that leaves her mostly absent?

SCENE 9

PROCNE *and the* FEMALE CHORUS.

HERO: Sometimes I feel I know things but I cannot prove that I
know them or that what I know is true and when I doubt
my knowledge it disintegrates into a senseless jumble of
possibilities, a puzzle that will not be reassembled, the
spider web in which I lie, immobile, and truth paralysed.

HELEN: Let me put it another way: I have trouble expressing
myself. The world I see and the words I have do not
match.

JUNE: I am the ugly duckling of fact, so most of the time I try
to keep out of the way.

ECHO: Quiet. I shouldn't be here at all.

IRIS: But sometimes it's too much and I must speak. Procne.

PROCNE: What are you women muttering about this time?
Something gloomy, no doubt.

IRIS: Procne, we sense danger.

PROCNE: You always sense something, and when I ask you
what, you say you don't know, it hasn't happened yet, but
it will, or it might. Well, what is it now? What danger?
This place is safe. No marauding bands outside, no
earthquake, what? What?

HERO: I say danger, she thinks of earthquakes. Doesn't know
the first meaning of danger is the power of a lord or master.

HELEN: That one is always in someone's danger.

ECHO: In their power, at their mercy.

JUNE: All service is danger and all marriage too.

IRIS: Procne, listen to me.

PROCNE: What now?

HERO: The sky was so dark this morning . . .

PROCNE: It'll rain. It always rains.

IRIS: Again.

HERO: I was not talking meteorologically. Images require sympathy.

ECHO: Another way of listening.

IRIS: Procne.

PROCNE: Yes, yes, yes.

HERO: Your sister is on the sea.

PROCNE: She's been on the sea for a month. Have you just found that out?

HELEN: But the sea, the sea . . .

HERO: And Tereus is a young man.

ECHO: Tereus.

PROCNE: He'll move that much more quickly. Tell me something I don't know.

HERO: When it's too late, it's easy to find the words.

IRIS: Procne.

PROCNE: Leave me alone.

IRIS: If you went down to the seaport. Met them there.

ECHO: A welcome . . .

PROCNE: I promised Tereus I would stay here and look after his country. I will wait for him here.

IRIS: Procne.

PROCNE: Enough of your nonsense. Be silent.

HELEN: Silent.

ECHO: Silent.

SCENE 10

The MALE CHORUS, FIRST SOLDIER, SECOND SOLDIER, TEREUS.

MALE CHORUS: We camp on a desolate beach. Days pass.

FIRST SOLDIER: Why are we still here?

SECOND SOLDIER: Tereus has his reasons.

FIRST SOLDIER: I want to go home.

SECOND SOLDIER: We can't until we have the order.

FIRST SOLDIER: It's no more than four days' walk to the palace. Why are we still here?

SECOND SOLDIER: I told you: because we haven't been ordered to move.

FIRST SOLDIER: Why not?

SECOND SOLDIER: You ask too many questions.

MALE CHORUS: Questions. The child's instinct suppressed in the adult.

MALE CHORUS: For the sake of order, peace.

MALE CHORUS: But at what price?

MALE CHORUS: I wouldn't want to live in a world that's always shifting. Questions are like earthquakes. If you're lucky, it's just a rumble.

FIRST SOLDIER: Why don't we ask Tereus if we can go home? I want to see my girl.

SECOND SOLDIER: He wants to see his wife.

FIRST SOLDIER: How do you know?

SECOND SOLDIER: He would, wouldn't he?

FIRST SOLDIER: Then why are we here?

SECOND SOLDIER: Ask him.

FIRST SOLDIER: Why don't you?

MALE CHORUS: More days pass. We all wait.

FIRST SOLDIER: Why don't we talk to him together? Respectful, friendly.

SECOND SOLDIER: And say what?

FIRST SOLDIER: Ask him if he's had any news of home. Tell him how nice it is. And spring's coming.

SECOND SOLDIER: I'd leave out the bit about spring.

FIRST SOLDIER: Why?

SECOND SOLDIER: Ready?

(*Pause.*)

Not today. He's worried.

FIRST SOLDIER: What about me?

SECOND SOLDIER: You're not a king. His worry is bigger than yours.

FIRST SOLDIER: Why?

SECOND SOLDIER: It's more interesting.

MALE CHORUS: Days.

MALE CHORUS: Days.

SECOND SOLDIER: Tereus?

TEREUS: Yes.

SECOND SOLDIER: He wants to speak to you.

TEREUS: Speak.

FIRST SOLDIER: Speak.

SECOND SOLDIER: Euh.

>   (*Pause.* TEREUS *turns away.*)

FIRST SOLDIER: Why are we here?

SECOND SOLDIER: What are we waiting for?

FIRST SOLDIER: Why aren't we going home?

SECOND SOLDIER: Why haven't any messengers been sent to tell everyone we're safe?

FIRST SOLDIER: We want to go home.

SECOND SOLDIER: We've had enough.

>   (*Pause.*)

TEREUS: I have my reasons.

MALE CHORUS: An old phrase, but it buys time. More days.

FIRST SOLDIER: What reasons?

SECOND SOLDIER: Yes, what reasons?

TEREUS: You must trust me.

>   (*Pause.*)
>
>   Am I not your leader?

SECOND SOLDIER: Yes, Tereus, but –

TEREUS: My knowledge is greater than yours, that is my duty, just as yours is to trust me. Think: when you fight wars with me, you see only part of the battle, the few enemies you kill, or your own wounds. Sometimes this seems terrible to you, I know, but later you see the victory and the glory of your country. That glory, fame, I have seen all along.

SECOND SOLDIER: Yes, Tereus, but.

FIRST SOLDIER: Where's the enemy?

TEREUS: I have information.

23

MALE CHORUS: More days.

SECOND SOLDIER: Why do we have to wait so long?

FIRST SOLDIER: For what?

SECOND SOLDIER: It's this waiting makes me afraid. I'd rather
something happened, anything.

TEREUS: I know this is difficult for you. (*Pause.*) It's difficult
for me. (*Pause.*) You're experienced soldiers, responsible
citizens, I trust you not to risk the safety and honour of
your country because you don't understand yet. Trust me
and you'll understand all in time.

MALE CHORUS: In time . . .

MALE CHORUS: What hasn't been said and done in the name of
the future? A future always in someone else's hands. We
waited, without the pain of responsibility for that promised
time, the good times. We asked no more questions and at
night, we slept soundly, and did not see:

SCENE II

PHILOMELE, NIOBE, TEREUS.

TEREUS: Philomele.

PHILOMELE: (*To* NIOBE) Why does he follow me everywhere?
Even Procne left me alone sometimes.

NIOBE: Don't make him angry!

PHILOMELE: Let's ignore him.

TEREUS: Philomele.

PHILOMELE: It's spring. Look at these flowers, Niobe, we have
them in the woods near Athens. I'll bring some to Procne.

TEREUS: Philomele.

PHILOMELE: And here is some wild thyme, and that is xorta.
Procne loves its bitter taste.

TEREUS: Philomele.

PHILOMELE: What is this plant, Niobe? Smell it. It's salty, I've
never seen it before. Procne will know.

TEREUS: Philomele!

24

PHILOMELE: Quiet, brother, you're disturbing the butterflies.
Procne would not like that.

TEREUS: Procne. Procne. Procne is dead.

(*Silence.*)

There is a mountain not far from the palace. She climbed it
with her women to see if she could catch sight of the sea.
On a clear day you can look at the sea from there. She
climbed to the top, but there was a tall rock and she said
she would climb that as well, to see us, to welcome the
ship. The women begged her not to, no one would follow
her. The rock is slippery and on the other side drops
straight into the river below. She climbed, climbed higher
to welcome her sister and stood there, waving, safe, the
women thought. But then she seemed to grow dizzy, she
cried out and suddenly fell, down the rock, down the cliff,
into the river swollen now because of the winter rains.
They are still looking for her body, it was carried with the
torrent. Perhaps better not to find it.

NIOBE: Yes, better. Never look at a battered body, it is worse
than the death that came to it.

TEREUS: Mourn, Philomele, mourn with me. She was my wife.

PHILOMELE: Procne.

TEREUS: Procne.

NIOBE: Procne.

(PHILOMELE *begins to cry and scream.* TEREUS *takes her in
his arms.*)

TEREUS: Sister, beloved sister. My sister.

PHILOMELE: Procne. No!

I want to see her body!

CHORUS: Nor did we see, still sleeping:

SCENE 12

PHILOMELE, *the* CAPTAIN, NIOBE.

PHILOMELE: How long have we been in this place forsaken by
the gods, Captain?

THE LOVE OF THE NIGHTINGALE

CAPTAIN: Almost a full month, Philomele.

PHILOMELE: Why?

    (*Pause.*)

    I can't mourn my sister here. Let me at least remember her where she lived all those years. Why do we wait and wait, for what?

CAPTAIN: There may be trouble. Tereus keeps these things to himself.

PHILOMELE: And you, Captain, where will you go?

CAPTAIN: I'm waiting for orders.

PHILOMELE: South?

CAPTAIN: Perhaps.

PHILOMELE: You won't say, you've been asked not to say, why?

CAPTAIN: You ask too many questions, Philomele.

PHILOMELE: And you ask none, why?

    (*Pause.*)

    Do you love the sea?

CAPTAIN: Sometimes.

PHILOMELE: I used to watch you at night, standing on your deck, an immense solitude around you. You seemed a king of elements, ordering the wind.

CAPTAIN: No, you guess the wind, you order the sails. The winds have names, they're godlike, man obeys.

PHILOMELE: I never understood obedience, Captain philosophical.

CAPTAIN: You're a woman.

PHILOMELE: Does that make me lawless? Do you have a wife?

CAPTAIN: No, no.

PHILOMELE: Why not?

NIOBE: (*Muttering*) Girl without shame. After a captain when she could have a king.

PHILOMELE: Take me with you.

CAPTAIN: Take you. Where?

PHILOMELE: On the sea. South . . . Wherever . . .

CAPTAIN: You're laughing at me, Philomele. Tereus . . .

26

PHILOMELE: Frightens me. Since Procne's accident. Perhaps
before. His eyes wander, have you noticed? In Athens the
philosophers used to talk about wandering eyes. I forget
exactly what they said, but it was not good. Yes, the eyes
are the windows of the soul – Tereus has a nervous soul.

CAPTAIN: You shouldn't speak like that. Not to me. My job is
to obey him.

PHILOMELE: Again! What about your obedience to the
elements, and desire, isn't that a god too?

CAPTAIN: Philomele . . .

PHILOMELE: You touched my hand on the ship once, by
mistake, and once I fell against you, a wave, you blushed, I
saw it, fear, desire, they're the same, I'm not a child.
Touch my hand again: prove you feel nothing.
(*She holds out her hand. The* CAPTAIN *hesitates and touches it.*)

PHILOMELE: So – I was right. Take me with you.

CAPTAIN: We will ask Tereus.

PHILOMELE: We will ask the gods within us. Love . . .

CAPTAIN: . . . your power . . .

PHILOMELE: Not mine . . . Between us, above us.
(*She takes his hand and puts it on her breast.* TEREUS *enters.*)

TEREUS: Traitor! Traitor! Traitor!
(*He kills the* CAPTAIN.)
A young girl, defenceless.
I'll cut off your genitals.
Go to the underworld with your shame around your neck.
(*Pause.*)
Be more careful, Philomele.

MALE CHORUS: (*Carrying the body off*) We saw nothing.

SCENE 13

Moonlight. The beach. PHILOMELE.

PHILOMELE: Catch the moonlight with your hands. Tread the
moonlight with your toes, phosphorescence,

phosphorescence, come to me, come to me, tell me the
secrets of the wine-dark sea.
(*Pause.*)
I am so lonely.
(*Pause.*)
Procne, come to me.
(*Pause. She waits.*)
Procne, Procne, sister. Help me.
Catch the lather of the moonlight. Spirits, talk to me.
Oh, you gods, help me.
(TEREUS *enters.* PHILOMELE *senses this.*)
(*Softly*) Phosphorescence, phosphorescence, tell me the
secrets of the wine-dark sea . . .
TEREUS: (*Softly*) Philomele, what are you doing?
PHILOMELE: Catching the lather of the sea. Moonlight,
moonlight.
TEREUS: I only wish you well . . .
PHILOMELE: Let me bury my sister.
TEREUS: I told you, we never found the body.
PHILOMELE: Take me to the gorge, I will find it.
TEREUS: Nothing left now, weeks –
PHILOMELE: I will find the bones.
TEREUS: Washed by the river.
PHILOMELE: Let me stand in the river.
TEREUS: It's dangerous.
PHILOMELE: I don't want to stay here.
TEREUS: You have everything you want, you loved the spot
when we first came.
PHILOMELE: Then . . .
Tereus, I want to see my sister's home, I want to speak to
the women who were with her. I want to know the last
words she said, please, please take me there. Why are we
here? What is the point of talking if you won't answer that
question?
(*Silence.* PHILOMELE *turns away.*)
Moonlight, moonlight . . .
TEREUS: Philomele, listen to me.

28

PHILOMELE: Light the shells, light the stones, light the dust of
old men's bones . . .

TEREUS: Philomele!

PHILOMELE: Catch the lather of the sea . . .

TEREUS: Do you remember that day in the theatre in Athens?
The play?

PHILOMELE: Evanescence, evanescence . . .

TEREUS: Philomele, I am telling you.

(*Pause.*)

I love you.

PHILOMELE: I love you too, brother Tereus, you are my sister's
husband.

TEREUS: No, no. The play. I am Phaedra. (*Pause.*) I love you.
That way.

(*Silence.*)

PHILOMELE: It is against the law.

TEREUS: My wife is dead.

PHILOMELE: It is still against the law.

TEREUS: The power of the god is above the law. It began then,
in the theatre, the chorus told me. I saw the god and I
loved you.

PHILOMELE: Tereus.

(*Pause.*)

I do not love you.

I do not want you.

I want to go back to Athens.

TEREUS: Who can resist the gods? Those are your words.
Philomele. They convinced me, your words.

PHILOMELE: Oh, my careless tongue. Procne always said – my
wandering tongue. But, Tereus, it was the theatre, it was
hot, come back to Athens with me. My parents – Tereus,
please, let me go back to Athens.

TEREUS: The god is implacable.

PHILOMELE: You are a king, you are a widower. This is –
frivolous.

TEREUS: You call this frivolous.

(*He seizes her.*)

PHILOMELE: Treachery.

TEREUS: Love me.

PHILOMELE: No.

TEREUS: Then my love will be for both. I will love you and love myself for you. Philomele, I will have you.

PHILOMELE: Tereus. Wait.

TEREUS: The god is out.

PHILOMELE: Let me mourn.

TEREUS: Your darkness and your sadness make you all the more beautiful.

PHILOMELE: I have to consent.

TEREUS: It would be better, but no, you do not have to. Does the god ask permission?

PHILOMELE: Help. Help me. Someone. Niobe!

TEREUS: So, you are afraid. I know fear well. Fear is consent. You see the god and you accept.

PHILOMELE: Niobe!

TEREUS: I will have you in your fear. Trembling limbs to my fire.

(*He grabs her and leads her off.* NIOBE *appears.*)

NIOBE: So it's happened. I've seen it coming for weeks. I could have warned her, but what's the point? Nowhere to go. It was already as good as done. I know these things. She should have consented. Easier that way. Now it will be all pain. Well I know. We fought Athens. Foolish of a small island but we were proud. The men – dead. All of them. And us. Well – we wished ourselves dead then, but now I know it's better to live. Life is sweet. You bend your head. It's still sweet. You bend it even more. Power is something you can't resist. That I know. My island bowed its head. I came to Athens. Oh dear, oh dear, she shouldn't scream like that. It only makes it worse. Too tense. More brutal. Well I know. She'll accept it in the end. Have to. We do. And then. When she's like me she'll wish it could happen again. I wouldn't mind a soldier. They don't look at me now. All my life I was afraid of them and then one day they stop looking and it's even more frightening. Because what

makes you invisible is death coming quietly. Makes you
pale, then unseen. First, no one turns, then you're not
there. Nobody goes to my island any more. It's dead too.
Countries are like women. It's when they're fresh they're
wanted. Why did the Athenians want our island? I don't
know. We only had a few lemon trees. Now the trees are
withered. Nobody looks at them. There. It's finished now.
A cool cloth. On her cheeks first. That's where it hurts
most. The shame. Then we'll do the rest. I know all about
it. It's the lemon trees I miss, not all those dead men.
Funny, isn't it? I think of the lemon trees.

SCENE 14

The palace of Tereus. PROCNE *and the* FEMALE CHORUS.

PROCNE: If he is dead then I want to see his body and if he is
   alive then I want to see him. That is logical. Iris, come
   here. Closer. There.
   (*Pause.*)
   Iris, I have seen you look at me with some kindness. You
   could be my friend, possibly? What is a friend? A friend
   tells the truth. Will you be my friend? No, don't turn
   away, I won't impose the whole burden of this friendship.
   One gesture, one gift. One question. Will you be my friend
   to the tune of one question? Ah, you don't say no. Iris,
   answer me. Is Tereus dead?
   (*Pause.*)
   Iris, please, pity. One yes, one no. Small words and yet can
   turn the world inside out.
   (*Pause.*)
   I have learned patience. It is the rain.
   (*Pause.*)
   The inexorable weight of a grey sky. I can wait.
   (*Silence.*)
   It's only one word.

31

Very well, don't. And when I kill myself, it will be for you
to bring news of my death, Iris. You don't believe me?
Athenians don't kill themselves. But I can be Thracian too.
I have been here long enough. Go now.

IRIS: No.

PROCNE: He is not dead.

IRIS: No.

PROCNE: But then, why?

(*Pause.*)

Yes, my promise. (*Pause.*) Thank you.

My sister? No, of course, another question. If there is one,
might there not be two? (*She addresses the women.*) My
husband is not dead. Who will tell me where he is? Why?
You have husbands among his men. Don't you ask
yourselves questions? What sirens have entangled them in
what melodies? Is that it? But no, he is not dead, so he is
not drowned. Turned into a wild beast by the power of a
witch, is that it? You've heard barking in the forest and
recognized your husbands? Don't dare say, the shame of it;
my husband is a dog. All fleas, wagging tail and the
irrational bite, well, is that it?

Weeks, weeks and no one speaks to me.

(*Pause.*)

Even a rumour would do.

Where are your men?

Where is mine?

Where is Tereus?

(TEREUS *and the* MALE CHORUS *enter.*)

TEREUS: Here.

(*Pause.*)

A delay.

PROCNE: (*Very still*) A delay.

(*Pause.*)

There's blood on your hands.

TEREUS: A wild beast. Or a god in disguise. Unnameable.

PROCNE: My sister?

TEREUS: (*After a brief pause*) Not here.

32

PROCNE: No. (*Pause.*) Drowned?
  (*Pause.*)
TEREUS: But I am here.
PROCNE: Yes.
  (*She opens her arms. The* MALE CHORUS *comes forward, hiding* TEREUS *and* PROCNE.)
MALE CHORUS: Home at last.
MALE CHORUS: We said nothing.
MALE CHORUS: It was better that way.

SCENE 15

PHILOMELE, NIOBE. PHILOMELE *is being washed by* NIOBE, *her legs spread out around a basin. Her head is down.*

NIOBE: There. Nothing left. It's a weak liquid, it drops out quickly. Not like resin.
PHILOMELE: I can still smell it. Wash me.
NIOBE: It's your own smell, there's nothing left.
PHILOMELE: It's the smell of violence. Wash me.
NIOBE: It's the smell of fear.
PHILOMELE: Wash me.
NIOBE: Some women get to like the smell. I never did. Too much like fishing boats. I like the smell of pines.
PHILOMELE: I want to die. Wash me.
NIOBE: You will, when it's time. In the meantime, get him to provide for you. They don't like us so much afterwards, you know. Now he might still feel something. We must eat. Smile. Beg.
PHILOMELE: Beg? Was it my fault?
NIOBE: I don't ask questions. Get some coins if you can.
PHILOMELE: Goddesses, where were you?
NIOBE: Stop worrying about the gods and think of us. Don't make him angry. He might still be interested. That would be excellent.
PHILOMELE: You. You are worse than him.

(*She pours the dirty water over* NIOBE.)

Filth. Here. Drink his excretions.

NIOBE: Don't be so mighty, Philomele. You're nothing now. Another victim. Grovel. Like the rest of us.

PHILOMELE: No.

NIOBE: Be careful. Worse things can happen. Keep low. Believe me. I know. Keep silent.

PHILOMELE: Never.

NIOBE: Here's the King. Hold back your tongue, Philomele.

(TEREUS *enters*.)

TEREUS: Now I wish you didn't exist.

(*Pause*.)

PHILOMELE: When will you explain, Tereus?

TEREUS: Explain?

PHILOMELE: Why? The cause? I want to understand.

TEREUS: I don't know what to do with you . . .

PHILOMELE: Me . . .

(*Pause*.)

I was the cause, wasn't I? Was I? I said something. What did I do?

(*Pause*.)

Something in my walk? If I had sung a different song? My hair up, my hair down? It was the beach. I ought not to have been there. I ought not to have been anywhere. I ought not to have been . . . at all . . . then there would be no cause. Is that it? Answer.

TEREUS: What?

PHILOMELE: My body bleeding, my spirit ripped open, and I am the cause? No, this cannot be right, why would I cause my own pain? That isn't reasonable. What was it then, tell me, Tereus, if I was not the cause?

(*Pause*.)

You must know, it was your act, you must know, tell me, why, say.

(*Pause*.)

It was your act. It was you. I caused nothing.

(*Short pause*.)

34

And Procne is not dead. I can smell her on you.
(*Pause.*)
You. You lied. And you.
What did you tell your wife, my sister, Procne, what did
you tell her? Did you tell her you violated her sister, the
sister she gave into your trust? Did you tell her what a
coward you are and that you could not, cannot bear to look
at me? Did you tell her that despite my fear, your violence,
when I saw you in your nakedness I couldn't help laughing
because you were so shrivelled, so ridiculous and it is not
the way it is on the statues? Did you tell her you cut me
because you yourself had no strength? Did you tell her I
pitied her for having in her bed a man who could screech
such quick and ugly pleasure, a man of jelly beneath his
hard skin, did you tell her that?
(*Pause.*)
And once I envied her happiness with her northern hero.
The leader of men. Take the sword out of your hand, you
fold into a cloth. Have they ever looked at you, your
soldiers, your subjects?

TEREUS: That's enough.

PHILOMELE: There's nothing inside you. You're only full when
you're filled with violence. And they obey you? Look up to
you? Have the men and women of Thrace seen you naked?
Shall I tell them? Yes, I will talk.

TEREUS: Quiet, woman.

PHILOMELE: You call this man your king, men and women of
Thrace, this scarecrow dribbling embarrassed lust, that is
what I will say to them, you revere him, but have you
looked at him? No? You're too awed, he wears his cloak of
might and virility with such ease you won't look beneath.
When he murdered a virtuous captain because a woman
could love that captain, that was bravery, you say. And if,
women of Thrace, he wants to force himself on you, trying
to stretch his puny manhood to your intimacies, you call
that high spirits? And you soldiers, you'll follow into a
battle a man who lies, a man of tiny spirit and shrivelled

courage? Wouldn't you prefer someone with truth and
goodness, self-control and reason? Let my sister rule in his
place.

TEREUS: I said that was enough.

PHILOMELE: No, I will say more. They will all know what you
are.

TEREUS: I warn you.

PHILOMELE: Men and women of Thrace, come and listen to the
truth about this man –

TEREUS: I will keep you quiet.

PHILOMELE: Never, as long as I have the words to expose you.
The truth, men and women of Thrace, the truth –

(TEREUS *cuts out* PHILOMELE'*s tongue*.)

SCENE 16

PHILOMELE *crouched in a pool of blood*. NIOBE.

NIOBE: Now truly I pity Philomele. She has lost her words, all
of them. Now she is silent. For good. Of course, he could
have killed her, that is the usual way of keeping people
silent. But that might have made others talk. The silence of
the dead can turn into a wild chorus. But the one alive who
cannot speak, that one has truly lost all power. There. I
don't know what she wants. I don't know what she feels.
Perhaps she likes being silent. No responsibility.

(PHILOMELE *seizes her, tries to express something*.)

I don't know what she wants. She can no longer command
me. What good is a servant without orders? I will go. I
don't know what she wants.

(TEREUS *enters*. PHILOMELE *stands still. Silence*.)

TEREUS: You should have kept quiet.

(*Pause*.)

I did what I had to.

(*Pause*.)

You threatened the order of my rule.

(*Pause.*)
How could I allow rebellion? I had to keep you quiet. I am
not sorry. Except for your pain. But it was you or me.
(*Long pause.*)
You are more beautiful now in your silence. I could love
you. You should have allowed the god to have his way. You
should have kept quiet. I was the stronger. And my desire.
Niobe, you will look after her. This to ease the pain. (*He
gives* NIOBE *money, then goes to* PHILOMELE) Why weren't
you more careful? Let me kiss those bruised lips. You are
mine. My sweet, my songless, my caged bird.
(*He kisses her. She is still.*)

SCENE 17

Tereus's palace. PROCNE, ITYS, TEREUS.

PROCNE: I wouldn't want to be young again. Time flows so
    gently as you get older. It used to feel broken by rocks.
    Five years since my sister died. Tomorrow. I will light a
    candle towards the sea, as I do every year. But the pain
    flickers now, almost out. Will you come with me this time,
    Tereus?
TEREUS: No.
PROCNE: I used to be angry that you would not mourn my
    sister. Why should you mourn her? You hardly knew her.
    Your aunt, Itys. You would have liked her. She was full of
    laughter.
ITYS: I have uncles. They're strong.
PROCNE: She could speak with the philosophers. She was bold
    and quick.
ITYS: What's a philosopher?
PROCNE: A man who loves wisdom.
ITYS: What is wisdom?
PROCNE: It brings peace.
ITYS: I don't like peace. I like war.

PROCNE: Why?

ITYS: So I can be brave. I want to be a great captain. Lead thousands into battle. Like Mars.

PROCNE: Mars is a god.

ITYS: What is a god?

PROCNE: Like us. But doesn't die.

ITYS: Why can't I be a god?

PROCNE: You have to be born one.

TEREUS: But you'll be a king, Itys. That's almost as good.

PROCNE: A wise king, like your father.

ITYS: (*Turning round with his spear in hand*) I'll fight this way. I'll fight that way. I'll fight this way. I'll fight this way. (*He runs out.*)

PROCNE: I am happy, as there was to be only one, that we have a son.
(*Pause.*)
Aren't you?

TEREUS: Yes.

PROCNE: You're quiet.
(*Pause.*)
Over the years you have become quiet. I used to be afraid of you, did you know? But we shall grow old in peace. I wish more people came to visit this country. Then we could show our hospitality. No one comes here. Why?
(*Silence.*)
And if a god came to visit, he would find us sitting here, content, and perhaps turn us into two trees as a reward, like Baucis and Philemon. Would you like that?

TEREUS: Not yet.

PROCNE: Ha. I love to see you smile.
(*Pause.*)
And tomorrow is the feast of Bacchus. I will go out this time. I will go out with the women of this country. You see how I become Thracian.
(*Pause.*)
You're going? Of course, you must. The evening is soft, look, stars too. We do not have many evenings together. I

was frightened of your evenings when we were first
married. That is why I sent you to Athens for my sister.
I am a woman now. I can take pleasure in my husband.
(*She approaches* TEREUS, *but he puts her away from him and
leaves. When he is gone, she holds the bottom of her stomach.*)
Desire. Now. So late.
Oh, you gods, you are cruel.
Or, perhaps, only drunk.
(*She begins to dress as a Bacchae as does the* FEMALE CHORUS.
Music.)

SCENE 18

Music. The stage fills with BACCHAE. NIOBE *enters leading*
PHILOMELE, *who carries two huge dolls. Behind her, the*
SERVANT *carries a third doll.*

NIOBE: No place safe from the Bacchae. They run the city and
the woods, flit along the beach, no crevass free from the
light of their torches. Miles and miles of a drunken chain.
These people are savages. Look at their women. You never
see them and when you do, breasts hanging out, flutes to
their mouths. In my village, they'd be stoned. Out of the
way, you, out of the way.
SERVANT: We could move faster without those big dolls, Niobe.
NIOBE: She wouldn't go without them. Years she's been
sewing, making them, painting faces. Look. Childlike
pastime for her, what can I say? It's kept her still. And
she's quiet anyway. Tereus said, get her out, quickly, into
the city. She'll be lost there. Another madwoman, no one
will notice. Could have cut off her tongue in frenzied
singing to the gods. Strange things happen on these nights,
I have heard.
SERVANT: Very strange, Niobe. But she was better in the hut.
NIOBE: No. It gives her a little outing. She's only seen us and
the King for five years.

39

SERVANT: He doesn't come much any more.

NIOBE: No. They all dream of silence, but then it bores them.

SERVANT: Who is she, Niobe?

NIOBE: No one. No name. Nothing. A king's fancy. No more.

SERVANT: I feel pity for her, I don't know why.

NIOBE: Look, some acrobats. The idiot will like it. Look. Look. See the acrobats. Now that's like my village. Except I believe they're women. Shame on them. But still, no harm in watching.

(*She thrusts* PHILOMELE *to the front of a circle, watching. A crowd gathers around. The* ACROBATS *perform. Finish. As they melt back into the crowd, the empty space remains and* PHILOMELE *throws the dolls into the circle.* NIOBE *grabs one of them and tries to grab* PHILOMELE, *but she is behind the second doll. Since the dolls are huge, the struggle seems to be between the two dolls. One is male, one is female and the male one has a king's crown.*)

NIOBE: A mad girl, a mad girl. Help me.

(*But the crowd applauds, makes a wider circle and waits in silence. The rape is re-enacted in a gross and comic way, partly because of* NIOBE's *resistance and attempt to catch* PHILOMELE. PHILOMELE *does most of the work with both dolls. The crowd laughs.* PHILOMELE *then stages a very brutal illustration of the cutting of the female doll's tongue. Blood cloth on the floor. The crowd is very silent.* NIOBE *still. Then the* SERVANT *comes inside the circle, holding the third doll, a queen. At that moment,* PROCNE *also appears in the front of the crowd's circle. She has been watching. The Procne doll weeps. The two female dolls embrace.* PROCNE *approaches* PHILOMELE, *looks at her and takes her away. The dolls are picked up by the crowd and they move off. A bare stage for a second. Then* PROCNE *and* PHILOMELE *appear,* PROCNE *holding on to* PHILOMELE, *almost dragging her. Then she lets go.* PHILOMELE *stands still.* PROCNE *circles her, touches her. Sound of music very distant. Then a long silence. The sisters look at each other.*)

PROCNE: How can I know that was the truth?

(*Pause.*)

You were always wild. How do I know you didn't take him to your bed?

You could have told him lies about me, cut out your own tongue in shame. How can I know?

You won't nod, you won't shake your head. I have never seen him violent. He would not do this.

He had to keep you back from his soldiers. Desire always burnt in you. Did you play with his sailors? Did you shame us all? Why should I believe you?

(*She shakes* PHILOMELE.)

Do something. Make me know you showed the truth.

(*Pause.*)

There's no shame in your eyes. Why should I believe you? And perhaps you're not Philomele. A resemblance. A mockery in this horrible drunken feast. How can I know?

(*Silence.*)

But if it is true. My sister.

Open your mouth.

(PHILOMELE *opens her mouth, slowly.*)

To do this. He would do this.

(*Pause.*)

Is that what the world looks like?

(*Pause.*)

Justice. Philomele, the justice we learned as children, do you remember? Where is it? Come, come with me.

(*The* BACCHAE *give wine to* PROCNE *and* PHILOMELE.)

Do this.

(PHILOMELE *drinks.*)

Drink. Oh, we will revel. You, drunken god, help us. Help us.

(*They dance off with the* BACCHAE.)

SCENE 19

TWO SOLDIERS.

FIRST SOLDIER: It's almost dawn. Let's go.

SECOND SOLDIER: He said to stay by the palace until the sun was up.

FIRST SOLDIER: What is he afraid of? An invasion of Amazons? They're all in there.

SECOND SOLDIER: Our enemies know this is a strange night.

FIRST SOLDIER: I never liked this festival. All these drunken women. My girl's in there. And she'll never tell what happens. I tell her about the war. Well. Most of it. Let's go.

SECOND SOLDIER: We can't.

FIRST SOLDIER: There's no law on these nights.

SECOND SOLDIER: Do you want to look in?

FIRST SOLDIER: They'd kill us.

SECOND SOLDIER: That window, there. We could see through the shutters.

FIRST SOLDIER: It's supposed to be a mystery. A woman's mystery. That's what my girl says. Give me a break.

SECOND SOLDIER: You could sit on my shoulders. Make sure your girl's behaving.

FIRST SOLDIER: It's all women in there.

SECOND SOLDIER: It's all men in a war.

FIRST SOLDIER: You mean, she – they – no.

SECOND SOLDIER: Have a look.

FIRST SOLDIER: If she – I'll strangle her. So that's what a mystery is. Let me see.

(*The* FIRST SOLDIER *climbs on to the* SECOND SOLDIER'*s shoulder.*)

SECOND SOLDIER: Can you see?

FIRST SOLDIER: Steady.

SECOND SOLDIER: I'm holding your legs. Can you see?

FIRST SOLDIER: Yeah.

SECOND SOLDIER: Well?

FIRST SOLDIER: It's just a lot of women.

SECOND SOLDIER: We know that, stupid. What are they doing?

FIRST SOLDIER: Drinking.

SECOND SOLDIER: And?

FIRST SOLDIER: Oh.

SECOND SOLDIER: What?

FIRST SOLDIER: Oh, you gods.

SECOND SOLDIER: Well? What are they doing? Exactly? What?

FIRST SOLDIER: (*Jumping down, laughing*) Nothing.
   (*He does a dance with the* SECOND SOLDIER.)
   Dancing. Lots of wine. They've swords and lances.
   (ITYS *has appeared*.)
   What are you doing here?

ITYS: I saw you.

FIRST SOLDIER: No men, no boys on the street. Go home.

ITYS: I saw you looking.

SECOND SOLDIER: That's Itys. Tereus's son. Why aren't you asleep?

ITYS: I saw you. I'm going to tell my father when he gets back.

FIRST SOLDIER: Nothing wrong with looking.

ITYS: Mother said no one's to see.
   I'll tell her, she'll tell Father. He'll be angry.

SECOND SOLDIER: Don't you want to see?

ITYS: It's not allowed.

SECOND SOLDIER: Aren't you a prince? A king's son? You let women tell you what is and is not allowed?

ITYS: You shouldn't have looked.

FIRST SOLDIER: It's just women.

SECOND SOLDIER: Why don't you see for yourself? A king has to be informed.

FIRST SOLDIER: You can sit on my shoulders.

SECOND SOLDIER: Do you know how to sit on somebody's shoulders? Are you strong enough?

ITYS: Of course I know.

SECOND SOLDIER: You sure? It's difficult.

FIRST SOLDIER: We'll hold you.

SECOND SOLDIER: No, we won't. You have to climb all by yourself. Like a man. Can you do it?

ITYS: I'll show you.

(ITYS *climbs on the shoulders of the* SECOND SOLDIER.)

SECOND SOLDIER: Good. You'll make a soldier yet. You're too small to reach the window, aren't you?

ITYS: No, I'm not.

SECOND SOLDIER: I think you are.

(ITYS *stretches himself to the window and looks. Pause.*)

ITYS: Oh.

FIRST SOLDIER: Still dancing, the women?

ITYS: They drink more than my father.

FIRST SOLDIER: But only once a year.

ITYS: There's Mother.

FIRST SOLDIER: What is she doing?

ITYS: Why should I tell you?

SECOND SOLDIER: Quite right, boy. What about the other women?

ITYS: There's one I've never seen before. She looks like a slave. That's my sword. That slave girl. A slave, a girl slave holding my sword. Let me down.

SECOND SOLDIER: Where are you going?

ITYS: To stop them.

FIRST SOLDIER: No.

SECOND SOLDIER: Wait.

(ITYS *runs off.*)

FIRST SOLDIER: Let's go.

SECOND SOLDIER: Let me look. (*He climbs.*) He's there. They've stopped. They're looking at him. It's all right. Procne is holding him. Shows him to the slave girl. He looks up. They've all gone still. He laughs. Oh! (*The* SECOND SOLDIER *drops down.*)

FIRST SOLDIER: What happened?
SECOND SOLDIER: I'm drunk. I didn't see anything. It didn't
    happen. The god has touched me with madness. For
    looking. I'm seeing things. I didn't see anything. Nothing.
    Nothing. Nothing. Let's go. I didn't see anything. There's
    Tereus. I don't know anything. I wasn't here.
    (*They run off.*)

SCENE 20

The FEMALE CHORUS. PROCNE. PHILOMELE.

HERO: Without the words to demand.
ECHO: Or ask. Plead. Beg for.
JUNE: Without the words to accuse.
HELEN: Without even the words to forgive.
ECHO: The words that help to forget.
HERO: What else was there?
IRIS: To some questions there are no answers. We might ask
    you now: why does the Vulture eat Prometheus's liver? He
    brought men intelligence.
ECHO: Why did God want them stupid?
IRIS: We can ask: why did Medea kill her children?
JUNE: Why do countries make war?
HELEN: Why are races exterminated?
HERO: Why do white people cut off the words of blacks?
IRIS: Why do people disappear? The ultimate silence.
ECHO: Not even death recorded.
HELEN: Why are little girls raped and murdered in the car
    parks of dark cities?
IRIS: What makes the torturer smile?
HERO: We can ask. Words will grope and probably not find.
    But if you silence the question.
IRIS: Imprison the mind that asks.
ECHO: Cut out its tongue.
HERO: You will have this.

JUNE: We show you a myth.

ECHO: Image. Echo.

HELEN: A child is the future.

HERO: This is what the soldiers did not see.

    (ITYS *comes running in.*)

ITYS: That's my sword. Give me my sword.

PROCNE: Itys.

ITYS: Give me my sword, slave, or I'll kick you. Kill you all.
    Cut off your heads. Pick out your eyes.

    (ITYS *goes for* PHILOMELE. PROCNE *holds him.*

    PHILOMELE *still has the sword.* PHILOMELE *brings the sword
    down on his neck. The* FEMALE CHORUS *close in front.*

    TEREUS *enters.*)

TEREUS: It's daylight at last. The revels are over. Time to go
    home.

    (*Silence. No one moves.*)

    We're whitewashing the streets. All that wine. Poured like
    blood. It's time for you to go home.

    (*No one moves.*)

    Stupefied? You should hold your wine better. You've had
    your revels. Go on. Stagger home. Procne, tell your women
    to go home.

    (PHILOMELE *is revealed. Hands bloodied. There is a silence.*)

TEREUS: I had wanted to say.

PROCNE: Say what, Tereus?

TEREUS: If I could explain.

PROCNE: You have a tongue.

TEREUS: Beyond words.

PROCNE: What?

TEREUS: When I ride my horse into battle, I see where I am
    going. But close your eyes for an instant and the world
    whirls round. That is what happened. The world whirled
    round.

    (*Pause.*)

PROCNE: What kept you silent? Shame?

TEREUS: No.

PROCNE: What?

TEREUS: I can't say. There are no rules.

PROCNE: I obeyed all rules: the rule of parents, the rule of marriage, the rules of my loneliness, you. And now you say. This.

(*Long pause.*)

TEREUS: I have no other words.

PROCNE: I will help you find them.

(*The body of* ITYS *is revealed.*)

PROCNE: If you bend over the stream and search for your reflection, Tereus, this is what it looks like.

TEREUS: Itys. You.

PROCNE: I did nothing. As usual. Let the violence sweep around me.

TEREUS: She –

PROCNE: No. You, Tereus. You bloodied the future. For all of us. We don't want it.

TEREUS: Your own child!

PROCNE: Ours. There are no more rules. There is nothing. The world is bleak. The past a mockery, the future dead. And now I want to die.

TEREUS: I loved her. When I silenced her, it was from love. She didn't want my love. She could only mock, and soon rebel, she was dangerous.

I loved my country. I loved my child. You – this.

PROCNE: You wanted something and you took it. That is not love. Look at yourself. That is not love.

TEREUS: How could I know what love was? Who was there to tell me?

PROCNE: Did you ask?

TEREUS: Monsters. Fiends. I will kill you both.

(TEREUS *takes the sword of* ITYS. *The* FEMALE CHORUS *comes forward.*)

HERO: Tereus pursued the two sisters, but he never reached them. The myth has a strange end.

ECHO: No end.

IRIS: Philomele becomes a nightingale.

JUNE: Procne a swallow.

HELEN: And Tereus a hoopoe.
HERO: You might ask, why does the myth end that way?
IRIS: Such a transformation.
ECHO: Metamorphosis.
(*The birds come on.*)

SCENE 21

ITYS *and the birds.*

PHILOMELE: (*The Nightingale*) And now, ask me some more
    questions.
ITYS: I wish you'd sing again.
PHILOMELE: You have to ask me questions first.
    (*Pause.*)
ITYS: Do you like being a nightingale?
PHILOMELE: I like the nights and my voice in the night. I like
    the spring. Otherwise, no, not much, I never liked birds,
    but we were all so angry the bloodshed would have gone on
    forever. So it was better to become a nightingale. You see
    the world differently.
ITYS: Do you like being a nightingale more than being
    Philomele?
PHILOMELE: Before or after I was silenced?
ITYS: I don't know. Both.
PHILOMELE: I always felt a shadow hanging over me. I asked
    too many questions.
ITYS: You want me to ask questions.
PHILOMELE: Yes.
ITYS: Will you sing some more?
PHILOMELE: Later.
ITYS: Why doesn't Procne sing?
PHILOMELE: Because she was turned into a swallow and
    swallows don't sing.
ITYS: Why not?
PHILOMELE: Different job.

48

ITYS: Oh.
    (*Pause.*)
    I like it when you sing.
PHILOMELE: Do you understand why it was wrong of Tereus to cut out my tongue?
ITYS: It hurt.
PHILOMELE: Yes, but why was it wrong?
ITYS: (*Bored*) I don't know. Why was it wrong?
PHILOMELE: It was wrong because –
ITYS: What does wrong mean?
PHILOMELE: It is what isn't right.
ITYS: What is right?
    (*The Nightingale sings.*)
    Didn't you want me to ask questions?
    (*Fade.*)

THE GRACE OF MARY TRAVERSE

For John

If you are squeamish
Don't prod the beach rubble

Sappho
Translated from the Greek by Mary Barnard

It may well be that it is a mere fatuity, an indecency to debate of the definition of culture in the age of the gas-oven, of the arctic camps, of napalm. The topic may belong solely to the past history of hope. But we should not take this contingency to be a natural fact of life, a platitude. We must keep in focus its hideous novelty or renovation . . . The numb prodigality of our acquaintance with horror is a radical human defeat.

George Steiner, *In Bluebeard's Castle*

The Grace of Mary Traverse was first produced at The Royal Court Theatre on 17 October 1985 with the following cast:

MARY TRAVERSE	Janet McTeer
GILES TRAVERSE	Harold Innocent
MRS TEMPTWELL	Pam Ferris
LORD GORDON	Tom Chadbon
OLD WOMAN	Jonathan Phillips
SOPHIE	Eve Matheson
MR MANNERS	James Smith
BOY	Jonathan Phillips
MR HARDLONG	David Beames
LORD EXRAKE	Harold Innocent
ROBERT	Jonathan Phillips
OLD WOMAN	Pam Ferris
OLD WOMAN	Eve Matheson
JACK	David Beames
GUARD	Jonathan Phillips
SPY	James Smith
LOCKSMITH	Tom Chadbon
MAN	Tom Chadbon
Director	Danny Boyle
Designer	Kandis Cook
Lighting	Christopher Toulmin

Although this play is set in the eighteenth century, it is not a historical play. All the characters are my own invention and whenever I have used historical events such as the Gordon Riots I have taken great freedom with reported fact. I found the eighteenth century a valid metaphor, and I was concerned to free the people of the play from contemporary preconceptions.

The game of piquet in Act II, scene 4, was devised with the help of David Parlett.

T.W.

ACT ONE

SCENE I

The drawing room of a house in the City of London during the late eighteenth century. MARY TRAVERSE *sits elegantly, facing an empty chair. She talks to the chair with animation.* GILES TRAVERSE *stands behind and away from her.*

MARY TRAVERSE: Nature, my lord. (*Pause.*) It was here all the
time and we've only just discovered it. What is nature? No,
that's a direct question. Perhaps we will not exhaust nature
as easily as we have other pleasures for it is difficult to
imagine with what to replace it. And there's so much of it!
No, that's too enthusiastic. (*Short pause.*) How admirable of
you to have shown us the way, my lord, to have made the
grand tour of such a natural place as Wales. Ah, crags,
precipices, what awe they must strike in one's breas– in
one's spirit. Yes. And I hear Wales even has peasants. How
you must have admired the austerity of their lives, their
human nature a complement to the land's starkness.
Peasants too I believe are a new discovery. How delightful of
our civilization to shed light on its own dark and savage
recesses. Oh dear, is that blue-stockinged or merely
incomprehensible? When you said the other day that he who
is tired of London is tired of life, did you mean – but how
foolish of me. It was Doctor Johnson. Forgive the
confusion, you see there are so few men of wit about.
(*Pause.*) You were telling me how we are to know nature. Do
we dare look at it directly, or do we trust an artist's
imitation, a poet, the paintings of Mr Gainsborough.
Whirlpools. Trees. Primordial matter. Circling. Indeed. Oh.
(MARY *stops in a panic.* GILES TRAVERSE *clears his throat.*
MARY *talks faster.*)
You visited the salt mines? Ah, to hover over the depths in
a basket and then to plunge deep down into the earth, into
its very bowels.

59

GILES TRAVERSE: No, no, my dear, do not mention bowels. Especially after dinner.

MARY: To have no more than a fragile rope between oneself and utter destruction. How thrilling!

GILES: No, Mary. It shakes your frame with terror and you begin to faint.

MARY: I wouldn't faint, Papa. I'd love to visit a salt mine.

GILES: You are here not to express your desires but to make conversation.

MARY: Can desire not be part of a conversation?

GILES: No. To be agreeable, a young woman must make the other person say interesting things.

MARY: He hasn't said a word.

GILES: Ah, but he won't know that. Now faint, and even the most tongue-tied fop will ask how you are. That allows you to catch your breath and begin again.

MARY: How clever of you, Papa. And the rivers . . .

GILES: There's too much of this nature in your conversation.

MARY: It is what people are thinking about.

GILES: Sounds foreign. I shall bring it up at the next meeting of the Antigallican Society.

MARY: Oh Papa, I could come and explain –

GILES: You? Now move on to another subject. This is difficult: leave no gap, you must glide into it. Converse, Mary, converse.

MARY: I can't think what follows naturally from nature. Ah: I hear God is . . . no . . . I believe God –

GILES: Talk of God leads to silence, Mary.

MARY: The architecture of –

GILES: Too athletic. People might think you spend time out of doors.

MARY: Reason, they say . . . is that too Popish?

GILES: No, but a woman talking about reason is like a merchant talking about the nobility. It smacks of ambition. I overheard that in a coffee house. Good, isn't it?

MARY: But Papa you're always talking about lords and you're a merchant.

GILES: I am not. Not exactly. Who told you this?

MARY: I look out of the window and see coaches with your name.

GILES: Why gape out of the window when I've given you so much to see in the house? I have land. There are potteries on it, but that's acceptable. Lord Folly has mines on his. And it's not refined to look too closely at the source of one's wealth. Now, you have a Methodist preacher here and a rake there. Keep them from the weather.

MARY: Books? Preachers don't read. Music? That's for afternoon tea with the ladies. Drink? No . . .

GILES: It's obvious. Praise England: patriotism.

MARY: But Papa, you won't let me study politics. And I'd so like to.

GILES: Patriotism is to politics what the fart is to the digestion. Euh, you're not to repeat that, although it was said by a very grand lady. A duchess. Say something against the Americans and fop, fool, rattle, mathematician and gambler will easily add to it.

MARY: Are we at war with them yet? Have you made another brilliant speech?

GILES: Yes. I demonstrated logically that God gave us the colonies for the sole purpose of advantageous trade. We are interested in their raw materials but not in their ideas. Ambitious upstarts! We'll finish now, I'm going to the theatre.

MARY: Let me come with you, Papa, it will help my conversation.

GILES: There's no need to see a play to talk about it. I'll bring you the playbill. We'll continue tomorrow with repartee and do a little better, I hope.

MARY: Wouldn't I do better if I saw a little more of the world?

GILES: I'm afraid that's not possible. Don't be sad. You have tried today and I'll reward you with a kiss.

MARY: Thank you, Papa.

GILES: You are my brightest adornment, my dear. I want to be proud of my daughter.

MARY: Yes, Papa.

GILES: You are my joy and my hope.

MARY: But Papa –

GILES: A compliment must be received in silence, Mary. The French always protest at compliments, but that's because they're so tediously argumentative. Goodbye.

MARY: Goodbye, Papa.

SCENE 2

The drawing room. MARY, *alone, walks back and forth across the carpet. She stops occasionally and examines the area on which she has just stepped.*

MARY: Almost.

> (*She walks. Stops and examines.*)

Yes. Better.

> (*She walks again. Looks.*)

Ah. There.

> (*She walks faster now, then examines.*)

I've done it. See the invisible passage of an amiable woman.

> (*Pause.*)

It was the dolls who gave me my first lesson. No well-made doll, silk-limbed, satin-clothed, leaves an imprint. As a child I lay still and believed their weightlessness mine. Awkward later to discover I grew, weighed. Best not to move very much. But nature was implacable. More flesh, more weight. Embarrassment all around. So the teachers came. Air, they said. Air? Air. I waited, a curious child, delighted by the prospect of knowledge. Air. You must become like air. Weightless. Still. Invisible. Learn to drop a fan and wait. When that is perfected, you may move, slightly, from the waist only. Later, dare to walk, but leave no trace. Now my presence will be as pleasing as my step, leaving no memory. I am complete: unruffled landscape. I may sometimes be a little bored, but my manners are

excellent. And if I think too much, my feet no longer
betray this.
(*She walks.*)
What comes after, what is even more graceful than air?
(*She tries to tiptoe, then stamps the ground and throws down
her fan.*)
Damn!
(*She stands still and holds her breath.*)
Mrs Temptwell!
(MRS TEMPTWELL *comes on immediately. Short silence.*)
My fan.

MRS TEMPTWELL: It's broken.

MARY: I dropped it.

MRS TEMPTWELL: A bad fall, Miss Mary.

MARY: Pick it up, please.

    (MRS TEMPTWELL *does so, with bad grace.*)

MRS TEMPTWELL: I have work to do.

MARY: Bring me some hot milk.

MRS TEMPTWELL: I'll call the chambermaid.

MARY: Watch me, Mrs Temptwell. Do I look ethereal?

MRS TEMPTWELL: You do look a little ill, Miss Mary, yes.

MARY: You don't understand anything. I'm trying not to
breathe.

MRS TEMPTWELL: Your mother was good at that.

MARY: Was she?

MRS TEMPTWELL: Said it thickened the waist. She died of not
breathing in the end, poor thing, may she rest in peace, I'm
sure she does, she always did.

MARY: Could she walk on a carpet and leave no imprint?

MRS TEMPTWELL: She went in and out of rooms with no one
knowing she'd been there. She was so quiet, your mother,
it took the master a week to notice she was dead. But she
looked ever so beautiful in her coffin and he couldn't stop
looking at her. Death suits women. You'd look lovely in a
coffin, Miss Mary.

MARY: I don't need a coffin to look lovely, Mrs Temptwell.

MRS TEMPTWELL: No, some women don't even have to die,

they look dead already, but that doesn't work as well. It's better to be dead and look as if you'd been alive than the other way, if you get my meaning, as if you'd been dead all the time, quiet and dull.

MARY: I don't look like that.

MRS TEMPTWELL: Only when you've been reading.

MARY: Oh. Some books are dull. The Young Ladies' Conduct. Caesar's Wars.

MRS TEMPTWELL: It's a strange thing about books, they make the face go funny. I had an uncle who took to books. He went all grey. Then he went mad. May I go now?

MARY: Your uncle doesn't count. Books improve the mind. Am I not charming and witty?

(Silence.)

That girl in number fourteen, the one you keep telling me about, she must read.

MRS TEMPTWELL: Oh no, she's too busy sitting at her window, staring at everything.

MARY: Gaping? She must have nothing to look at in her own house, poor thing.

MRS TEMPTWELL: She even asked one of the servants to take her out on the street.

MARY: Outside? On foot? She did? Oh. But her reputation?

MRS TEMPTWELL: Disguised. No one will know. I wish you could see her, Miss Mary, she . . .

MARY: What?

MRS TEMPTWELL: Glitters with interest.

MARY: Glitters? How vulgar. Where's my milk?

MRS TEMPTWELL: Your mother wanted to go out once in her life, but she died before we could manage it. I felt sorry she missed that one little pleasure.

MARY: Papa wouldn't have been pleased.

MRS TEMPTWELL: The master doesn't see everything. I'll fetch your milk now.

MARY: What's so different out there? When I ride in my carriage I see nothing of interest.

MRS TEMPTWELL: That's because the streets have to be

emptied to make way for your carriage. It's different on
foot. Very different. Would you prefer a glass of ratafia?

MARY: Wait.

MRS TEMPTWELL: I haven't got all day.

MARY: What harm could once do? It'll only improve my
conversation and Papa will admire me. Yes, Mrs
Temptwell, you'll take me.

MRS TEMPTWELL: Take you where, Miss Mary?

MARY: You know very well. You'll take me out there. Yes. Into
the streets. I'll glitter with knowledge.

MRS TEMPTWELL: I can't do that, I'll lose my place.

MARY: We'll go disguised, as you suggested.

MRS TEMPTWELL: I didn't, Miss Mary, I never did.

MARY: I've decided, Mrs Temptwell, we're going out.

MRS TEMPTWELL: What have I done?

MARY: I'll pay you.

MRS TEMPTWELL: You always make me talk too much.

SCENE 3

Cheapside, London. LORD GORDON *comes on.*

LORD GORDON: My name is George Gordon. Lord Gordon.
(*Pause.*) Nothing. No reaction. No one's interested.
(*Pause.*) It's always like this. I greet people, their eyes
glaze. I ride in Hyde Park, my horse falls asleep. (*Pause.*) I
am a man of stunning mediocrity. (*Pause.*) This can't go
on. I must do something. Now. But what? How does Mr
Manners make everyone turn around? Of course: politics.
I'll make a speech in the House: all criminals must be
severely punished. But stealing a handkerchief is already a
hanging matter. I know: make England thrifty, enclose the
common land. I think that's been done. Starve the poor to
death! Perhaps politics is too ambitious. I'll write. Even
women do that now. But about what? No, I'll be a wit. I'll

make everyone laugh at what I say. But I'll have to think of
something funny. Sir John's a rake, that's a possibility. But
the ladies are so demanding and my manhood won't rise
above middling. Shall I die in a duel? No. This is
desperate. Perhaps I'm seen with the wrong people.
They're all so brilliant. In a different world, I might shine.
Here are some ordinary people. They must notice me, if
only because I'm a lord. Oh God, please make me noticed,
just once. Please show me the way.

(LORD GORDON *adopts an interesting pose. An* OLD WOMAN
walks on, very slowly.)

Hm.

(*She looks at him and continues walking.* SOPHIE *comes on.*)

SOPHIE: Please –

(*The* OLD WOMAN *turns around.*)

No, you're not . . . I'm sorry. I'm looking for someone
called Polly.

(*Pause.*)

My aunt . . . I'm to find her here. This is Cheapside?

(*The* OLD WOMAN *nods.*)

She has her pitch here. I've come to work for her. You
don't know where she is?

(*The* OLD WOMAN *shakes her head.*)

I'm not sure what she looks like. I haven't seen her for
such a long time. (*Pause.*) Where could she be?

(*The* OLD WOMAN *shrugs.*)

I don't know anyone.

(*The* OLD WOMAN *walks away.*)

What am I going to do?

(*The* OLD WOMAN *moves off.*)

London's so big.

LORD GORDON: Hhm.

(SOPHIE *looks briefly at him.*)

SOPHIE: I must find Aunt Polly.

(SOPHIE *goes off.* MARY *and* MRS TEMPTWELL *come on.*)

MARY: I believe I've just stepped on something unpleasant, Mrs
Temptwell. These streets are filthy.

66

MRS TEMPTWELL: The dirt runs out of great houses like yours.

MARY: What? I don't like this world. It's nasty.

MRS TEMPTWELL: If you're squeamish, don't stir the beach rubble.

MARY: What did you say?

MRS TEMPTWELL: It's a saying we had in our family.

MARY: Did you have a family? I can't imagine you anywhere but in our house.

MRS TEMPTWELL: Lack of imagination has always been a convenience of the rich.

LORD GORDON: Hhmm.

MARY: What? I do wish these people weren't so ugly.
    (*The* OLD WOMAN *comes on.*)

MRS TEMPTWELL: Their life is hard.

MARY: They ought to go back to the country and be beautiful peasants.

MRS TEMPTWELL: They've already been thrown off the land. Some of them were farmers.

MARY: Papa says farmers stop progress. I meant beautiful peasants I could talk about with grace. There's nothing here to improve my conversation.

MRS TEMPTWELL: It takes time to turn misery into an object of fun.

LORD GORDON: (*Louder.*) Hhmmm.

MARY: Why does that man keep clearing his throat?

MRS TEMPTWELL: I don't know. He doesn't look mad.

MARY: I want to go back.

MRS TEMPTWELL: So soon, Miss Mary? Such a dull appetite?

MARY: I might be curious about the plague and not care to embrace the dead bodies. This ugliness looks contagious. I'm going.

LORD GORDON: No. This is intolerable. You can't go without noticing me. My name is George Gordon. Lord Gordon.

MARY: Let's go.

LORD GORDON: How dare someone like you ignore me. You!

MARY: Mrs Temptwell, I'm frightened.

LORD GORDON: I don't want you to be frightened. Wait. Yes. Are you very frightened?

MARY: No, not very.

LORD GORDON: How dare you!

(*He takes out his sword.*)

Now. Now you're very frightened. I can see it. Why didn't I think of this before?

MARY: I want to go home.

LORD GORDON: Not yet. I'll make you even more frightened. Yes. I'll show you my strength. Come over here to the lamp-post.

MARY: Help! Mrs Temptwell!

MRS TEMPTWELL: This is the world.

(SOPHIE *comes on.*)

SOPHIE: Please —

MRS TEMPTWELL: Damn!

SOPHIE: Oh. I'm sorry . . . Have you by any chance seen my aunt? Her name's Polly . . . what's there?

MRS TEMPTWELL: Nothing for you, girl. Go away. Quickly.

SOPHIE: But he's —

MRS TEMPTWELL: So what? It could be you.

(SOPHIE *goes towards* LORD GORDON *and* MARY.)

SOPHIE: Leave her alone, Sir. What are you doing?

LORD GORDON: Everyone pays me attention now. Who are you? I'll have you too.

SOPHIE: No, Sir, please Sir. Please —

(LORD GORDON *grabs* SOPHIE. MARY *gets away.*)

LORD GORDON: Beg. Yes. Beg for mercy. Beg.

SOPHIE: Please have mercy, Sir.

LORD GORDON: What delight! Say over and over again Lord Gordon have mercy on me. Say it.

SOPHIE: Lord Gordon have mercy on me.

LORD GORDON: Again, again. On your knees and keep saying my name.

SOPHIE: Lord Gordon have mercy on me. Lord Gordon. Lord Gordon.

LORD GORDON: My strength rises. I can't contain myself. Over here.

MARY: Call for help, Mrs Temptwell.

MRS TEMPTWELL: Why?

MARY: What will he do to her?

MRS TEMPTWELL: Rape her. But she won't mind. Virtue, like ancestors, is a luxury of the rich. Watch and you'll learn something.

MARY: Rape? What the Greek gods did? Will he turn himself into a swan, a bull, a shower of golden rain? Is he a god?

MRS TEMPTWELL: He'll feel like one.

MARY: He stands her against the lamp-post, sword gleaming at her neck, she's quiet. Now the sword lifts up her skirts, no words between them, the sword is his voice and his will. He thrusts himself against her, sword in the air. He goes on and on. She has no expression on her face. He shudders. She's still. He turns away from her, tucks the sword away. I couldn't stop looking. (*Pause.*) It's not like the books. (MR MANNERS *comes on.*)

Sir, be careful, there's someone –

MR MANNERS: Go away, I only give money to organized charities. Lord Gordon. I was looking for you.

LORD GORDON: Mr Manners. I was just thinking of you.

MR MANNERS: Have I disturbed you?

LORD GORDON: Not at all. I'm finished.

MR MANNERS: Who are these women?

LORD GORDON: Just women. What shall we do tonight? I feel exceptionally lively.

MR MANNERS: We might play a game of piquet.

LORD GORDON: Yes. I'll win. My fortune has turned.

MR MANNERS: Delighted. Shall we have supper before?

LORD GORDON: I've never felt so hungry. Let's eat at a chop house.

MR MANNERS: There's something on at the Opera.

LORD GORDON: But first, let's go to a coffee house. I have some witticisms.

MR MANNERS: You, Lord Gordon?

LORD GORDON: Mr Manners, I'm a different man.

MR MANNERS: What's happened? A legacy?

LORD GORDON: (*Quietly*) Power.

MR MANNERS: Ah. Power.

LORD GORDON: Isn't power something you know all about?

MR MANNERS: Yes, but it is not something I ever discuss.

    (*They go.* SOPHIE *comes down towards* MARY *walking with pain. They look at each other. Then* SOPHIE *moves off.*)

MARY: (*Looking at the ground*) Blood.

SCENE 4

Outside the Universal Coffee House in Fleet Street. BOY, *an eighteenth-century waiter, blocks* MARY *and* MRS TEMPTWELL.

BOY: You can't.

MARY: They've just gone in.

BOY: You can't come in.

MARY: We're following them.

BOY: Ladies wait outside.

MRS TEMPTWELL: Ask him why.

BOY: They don't like to be disturbed.

MARY: I know how to talk.

BOY: They don't do ladies' talk.

MARY: What sex is wit?

MRS TEMPTWELL: Ask him who's in there.

BOY: Mr Fielding, Mr Goldsmith, Mr Hume, Mr Boswell,
    Mr Garrick, the Doctor, Mr Sheridan, Mr Hogarth.

MARY: But I know them all very well. I've often imagined
    talking to them. Let me in immediately.

BOY: And some foreigners, Mr Piranesis, Mr Tyepolo,
    Mr Hayden, Mr Voltaire, Mr Leibniz, Mr Wolfgang.
    They're quiet, the foreigners, and no one listens to them.
    You have to stay out. Orders.

MRS TEMPTWELL: Ask him why they let him in.

BOY: I'm the boy. I go everywhere.

MARY: I don't understand.

BOY: I'll let you see through the window.

MARY: I've spent my life looking through window panes. I want to face them.

BOY: Wouldn't be right.

MRS TEMPTWELL: Doesn't right belong to those who take it?

BOY: I don't ask questions.

MRS TEMPTWELL: Don't you wish you could be like him?

MARY: Yes. No. Envy is a sin, Mrs Temptwell.

MRS TEMPTWELL: And heaven must be a lady's tea party: the jingling of beatific stupidity.

MARY: What's happened to me? I was happy in my rooms.

MRS TEMPTWELL: Think of what you've seen.

MARY: I've seen them walk the streets without fear, stuff food into their mouths with no concern for their waists. I've seen them tear into skin without hesitation and litter the streets with their discarded actions. But I have no map to this world. I walk it as a foreigner and sense only danger.

BOY: I never stay anywhere long. There's too much to do.

MARY: Be quiet!

BOY: It's a waste of time being kind to women.

MARY: I'm going to hate you. No, that's an ugly feeling.

MRS TEMPTWELL: Why waste your time hating him, Mary? You could be like him if you wanted to. But there's a price.

BOY: Her soul.

MRS TEMPTWELL: We're not so medieval, boy. We're Protestants and the century's enlightened.

(*To* MARY) Do you want to travel in their world? Around every corner, the glitter of a possibility. You'll no longer be an ornate platter served for their tasting. No, you'll feast with them. No part of flesh or mind unexplored. No horizon ever fixed.

Experience! (*Pause.*) I could manage it for you.

BOY: We're not deceived when they dress as men. A lady came to us masqueraded. We uncovered her. All of her.

MRS TEMPTWELL: Do I sound so superficial? Well, Mary?

MARY: Run the world through my fingers as they do?

(*Pause.*)

Oh yes, I want it. Yes. What's the price?

MRS TEMPTWELL: You'll stay with me.

MARY: Yes, but the price?

MRS TEMPTWELL: You can never go back. (*Pause.*) Have they ever asked to live like us?

MARY: No, they're too busy. But I want the world as it is, Mrs Temptwell, no imitations, no illusions, I want to know it all.

MRS TEMPTWELL: You'll know all you want to know.

BOY: Will you sign a contract?

MRS TEMPTWELL: It's done. You can go back inside, boy.

BOY: It's more interesting out here this evening. May I stay?

MRS TEMPTWELL: See now, Mary, who's outside.

MARY: Yes. Yes. How will I pay you, Mrs Temptwell?

MRS TEMPTWELL: Don't worry. You'll pay.

ACT TWO

SCENE I

The Brothers Club. GILES TRAVERSE, MR MANNERS.

MR MANNERS: Three days?

GILES: Three.

MR MANNERS: And the letter?

GILES: Only that her dear Papa would understand, she'd gone to investigate the very underside of nature. I thought she meant Vauxhall Gardens. I don't approve of course, but Lord Oldland told me his daughter often went to Vauxhall, masked, and never came to any harm.

MR MANNERS: Have you told anyone?

GILES: No. I went to Bow Street.

MR MANNERS: My dear Giles, you might as well have gone straight to the papers.

GILES: It is my daughter, Manners. She could have been kidnapped.

MR MANNERS: This isn't France. You said she left with a servant. An elopement?

GILES: No. Manners, you must know someone who can investigate, discreetly.

MR MANNERS: No one in politics can afford the cost of a secret, Giles, not even you. No. There's nothing you can do. Forget her.

GILES: Forget my daughter!

MR MANNERS: Do you think most of the men in this club know where their children are. Or who they are, for that matter?

GILES: I have only one daughter.

MR MANNERS: You have only one country. The King, Giles, wants new men in the Cabinet. Men of intelligence and ambition, who show strength of character. There has been mention of you. But should there be a scandal . . .

GILES: The Cabinet. Now?

MR MANNERS: These are difficult times. I had the impression

73

you had a strong sense of duty. Perhaps I was wrong . . .

GILES: After all these years. Why now?

MR MANNERS: You of all people should know: supply and
demand. People have become suspicious of the old families.
But the old families do know how to conduct
themselves . . .

(LORD GORDON *comes on.*)

LORD GORDON: Giles. Just the man I was looking for.

GILES: My lord.

LORD GORDON: I have made a momentous decision. Yes. I've
decided to get married. It's what I need: a wife to look up
to me. I have decided to marry your daughter.

GILES: You've seen her!

LORD GORDON: How could I? You've never presented her. I
don't want to marry a woman I know. You've said your
daughter is pretty and clever. She's not too clever, is she?
She won't talk at breakfast? I couldn't bear that.

(*Silence.*)

She hasn't married someone else, has she? I'll kill him in a
duel. I wouldn't mind marrying a widow: less to explain.

MR MANNERS: Giles' daughter died yesterday, of a bad chill.

GILES: Mr Manners!

MR MANNERS: I know how painful it is for you, Giles. We
won't mention her again.

LORD GORDON: How inconvenient. I'll have to think of
something else. You don't have any other daughters, do
you?

GILES: No. Mr Manners, I –

MR MANNERS: At least she went quietly, Giles, we must be
thankful for that. I'll speak to the King, he may find a way
to ease your grief. Kings have such curative powers.

LORD GORDON: I think I'll be broken-hearted over your
daughter's death, Giles, it'll make me interesting.

SCENE 2

The study of GILES TRAVERSE. *He is in some disarray.* MRS
TEMPTWELL *is dressed for the street.*

GILES: Where is she?

MRS TEMPTWELL: Don't you know? You buried her.

GILES: Who are you?

MRS TEMPTWELL: I've been in your house for twenty-five
 years, Sir.

GILES: I know that, Mrs Temptwell. Why have you done this?

MRS TEMPTWELL: Done what, Sir? I've always done what
 Mary asked. She used to want cups of tea. Now she wants
 other things.

GILES: I'll have you thrown in prison.

MRS TEMPTWELL: For what? Killing her? I might have to tell
 people she's still alive. Think of the questions . . .

GILES: I trusted you with the care of my daughter. Was Mary
 not kind to you?

MRS TEMPTWELL: As she might be to the chair she sat on. She
 cared for my use.

GILES: What more can a servant expect?

MRS TEMPTWELL: Do you remember my father? He was a
 farmer when you were a farmer. His land was next to
 yours.

GILES: I must have bought it.

MRS TEMPTWELL: He trusted you to leave him his cottage.
 When you landscaped your garden, you needed a lake. The
 cottage was drowned in the lake.

GILES: I gave those people work.

MRS TEMPTWELL: He went to one of your potteries. He died.

GILES: And it's because of your father's misfortune that you've
 killed my daughter?

MRS TEMPTWELL: Your daughter's only dead for you. That's
 your misfortune.

GILES: Please tell me where she is.

MRS TEMPTWELL: She's not ready to see you. She hasn't yet learned to be a ghost.

GILES: I'll give you anything you want.

MRS TEMPTWELL: You've already done that.

GILES: I don't understand.

MRS TEMPTWELL: It's simple, Giles Traverse. When a man cries, he could be anybody.

SCENE 3

Lodgings in Marylebone. MRS TEMPTWELL *stands in the background and watches.* MARY *is fully dressed.* MR HARDLONG *is naked. They remain far apart.*

MR HARDLONG: You ask for pleasure. Why do you cringe as if expecting violence?

(*Short silence.*)

If you believe violence will bring you pleasure, you've been misled. The enjoyment of perversion is not a physical act but a metaphysical one. You want pleasure: come and take it.

(*Silence.* MARY *does not move.*)

Are you pretending you've never felt desire unfurl in your blood? Never known the gnawing of flesh, that gaping hunger of the body? Never sensed the warm dribble of your longings? Come, come, need isn't dainty and it's no good calling cowardice virginity.

(MARY *squirms a little.*)

Perhaps you want me to seduce you and let you remain irresponsible? I promised you physical pleasure, not the tickle of self-reproach and repentance, the squirm of the soul touching itself in its intimate parts. Or are you waiting for a declaration of love? Let romance blunt the sting of your need, mask a selfish act with selfless acquiescence? Novels, my dear, novels. And in the end, your body

76

remains dry. What are you waiting for? Pleasure requires
activity. Come.

(MARY *moves a little closer and closes her eyes*.)

Ah, yes. Close the eyes, let the act remain dark. Cling to
your ignorance, the mind's last chastity. A man's body is
beautiful, Mary, and ought to be known. I'll even give you
some advice, for free: never take a man you don't find
beautiful. If you have to close your eyes when he comes
near you, turn away, walk out of the room and never look
back. You may like his words, his promises, his wit, his
soul, but wrapping your legs around a man's talent will
bring no fulfilment. No, open your eyes. Look at me.

(MARY *looks, unfocused*.)

The neck is beautiful, Mary, but doesn't require endless
study. Look down. The arms have their appeal and the
hands hold promise. The chest can be charming, the ribs
melancholic. Look down still. They call these the loins,
artists draw their vulnerability, but you're not painting a
martyrdom. Look now.

(MARY *focuses on his penis*.)

See how delicate the skin, how sweetly it blushes at your
look. It will start at your touch, obey your least guidance.
It's one purpose is to serve you and you'd make it an object
of fear? Look, Mary, shaped for your delight, intricacies
for your play, here is the wand of your pleasure, nature's
generous magic. I'm here for you. Act now. You have
hands, use them. Take what you want, Mary. Take it.

(MARY *stretches out her hand*.)

MARY: At first, power. I am the flesh's alchemist. Texture
hardens at my touch, subterranean rivers follow my fingers.
I pull back the topsoil, skim the nakedness of matter. All
grows in my hand.

Now to my needs. Ouch! No one warned me about the
pain, not so pleasant that. Scratch the buttocks in
retaliation, convenient handles and at my mercy. And now
to the new world. Ah, but this is much better than
climbing mountains in Wales. I plunge to the peaks again

and again with the slightest adjustment. One, two, three, change of angle, change of feel. This is delightful and I'm hardly breathless. Again. Not Welsh this, the Alps at least: exploding sunshine, waterfalls, why is this geography not in the books? On to the rolling waves of the Bay of Biscay, I would go on forever, why have you stopped, Mr Hardlong, have you crashed on the Cape? You don't answer, Mr Hardlong, you're pale and short of breath. I am the owner of this mine and there are seams still untouched. You mustn't withdraw your labour. You seem a little dead, Mr Hardlong. I want more.

MRS TEMPTWELL: We'll have to find you someone else, Mary.

MARY: I like this one. I love you, Mr Hardlong, yes, I do. I thought I loved my father, but that was cold. This is hot. Don't turn away, Mr Hardlong, please don't die.

MRS TEMPTWELL: Don't be sentimental, labour's expendable.

MARY: He's reviving! Oh, joy!

MR HARDLONG: Where's my gold?

MARY: Here, Mr Hardlong, take it. And bring food to revive us, Mrs Temptwell. A duck, some good roast beef, and a pudding of bread and butter, very sweet. You'll eat with me, Mr Hardlong.

MR HARDLONG: I don't have time. Where is she?

MARY: Who?

MR HARDLONG: You promised she'd be here, Mrs Temptwell.

MRS TEMPTWELL: I haven't forgotten. (*She calls.*) Sophie!
(SOPHIE *comes on, bringing food.* MARY *pounces on it.*)

MARY: (*Eating*) I've seen you before. I remember now: Lord Gordon. I was sorry.

MRS TEMPTWELL: (*Touching* SOPHIE's *stomach*) Observe how mediocrity loves to duplicate itself. Take the rest of your payment, Mr Hardlong.

MR HARDLONG: (*To* SOPHIE) Come with me.

SOPHIE: Mrs Temptwell, you didn't tell me –

MRS TEMPTWELL: Do you want to starve on the streets?

MR HARDLONG: Don't be afraid, I won't hurt you.

SOPHIE: You said I was to work for a lady.

78

MRS TEMPTWELL: So you are. Mr Hardlong's price was high. You've saving Mary half her gold. That's what servants are for.

MR HARDLONG: Come quickly.

MARY: Mr Hardlong.

MR HARDLONG: Look. I have gold.

MARY: Mr Hardlong, please.

MR HARDLONG: What is it, Mary? You see I'm in a hurry.

MARY: At least answer one question. I paid you a good sum for what we did.

MR HARDLONG: Fifty guineas.

MARY: You'll give it to Sophie.

MR HARDLONG: All of it.

MARY: For the same thing we did?

MR HARDLONG: The same.

MARY: I pay you. You pay her. I don't understand.

MR HARDLONG: I gave you pleasure, Mary.

MARY: Yes. You did. Yes.

MR HARDLONG: Did you offer me any?

MARY: I confess I forgot a little about you. But weren't we doing the same thing?

MR HARDLONG: I had to look after your well-being.

MARY: You mean we were at the same table but I let you beg while I feasted? I see. But Sophie?

MR HARDLONG: Will serve my luxury.

MARY: I would do that too, Mr Hardlong. I would advocate the community of pleasure. Teach me what to do and I will.

MR HARDLONG: It's too late, Mary: you would have to learn to ask for nothing.

(MR HARDLONG *and* SOPHIE *go.* MARY *eats pensively, but none the less grossly.*)

MARY: Which do I like best? The first taste on the palate or the roast skin crinkling on the tongue? I like to swallow too. I'm still hungry.

(*She stops.*)

It's not really hunger, it's a void in the pit of my stomach. Knowledge scoops out its own walls and melancholy threatens. Yes, but I didn't have to leave my rooms to learn that nature abhors a void. What comes next, Mrs Temptwell, what comes next?

SCENE 4

A large den in Drury Lane. LORD EXRAKE *and* MR MANNERS *are playing piquet.* YOUNG ROBERT *is watching sulkily.* MARY, SOPHIE *and* MRS TEMPTWELL *come on.*

MR MANNERS: Carte blanche.
  (LORD EXRAKE *discards five cards.*)
MARY: Cards, numbers, chance, mystery and gain. Oh what a rich and generous world.
MRS TEMPTWELL: For some.
MARY: Don't be glum, Mrs Temptwell, let me enjoy it all.
LORD EXRAKE: Six and a *seizième*.
MARY: And look over there, a cock fight. Shall we go there or play cards? What do you want to do, Sophie?
SOPHIE: Me? . . . I don't know . . .
MRS TEMPTWELL: Our Sophie has no desires.
SOPHIE: Please . . .
YOUNG ROBERT: (*Moving towards* SOPHIE) What's your name?
MARY: But causes desires in others. I don't understand the world yet, but I will, I will.
MR MANNERS: You're over the hundred, Lord Exrake.
LORD EXRAKE: Am I, dear boy? So I am, so I am. Robert, why aren't you watching this?
ROBERT: I don't want to learn piquet, Uncle. I think cards are stupid.
LORD EXRAKE: What have you been doing at Oxford all this time?
ROBERT: Studying.
LORD EXRAKE: Whoever heard of studying at Oxford? Meet people, boy, meet people. Another deal, Mr Manners?

MARY: You play, Sophie, I'll go and watch the fight.

SOPHIE: I can't.

MARY: I'll give you the money and you can keep what you win.

SOPHIE: No . . .

MARY: Try a little pleasure, Sophie, do. Let's play cards.

MRS TEMPTWELL: Be careful.

MARY: Why?

ROBERT: (*To* SOPHIE) When I inherit his money, I'm going to build a school for women.

SOPHIE: Oh.

ROBERT: It will help all these lost girls find virtue and religion again. It's terrible what's happening to women now. I've written a play about it, but no one will put it on. There's a cabal against me and Garrick's a coward.

MR MANNERS: Piqued, repiqued and capoted. You have all the luck tonight, Lord Exrake.

LORD EXRAKE: At my age, dear boy, there is no luck, only science. (*He sees the women.*) Ah, look, beauties are approaching us. We are having a visitation, a visitation from the fair sex. Let us hail them.

(LORD EXRAKE *messes up the cards.*)

You owe me four hundred and fifty pounds.

MR MANNERS: Another deal, Lord Exrake, so I can win back some of my losses.

LORD EXRAKE: No, no, dear boy, don't win, don't win. *Qui perd au jeu gagne à l'amour*, and of course, vice versa. Do they still teach the young boys French? Ah, *l'amour*, *l'amour*, what good is gold without *l'amour*. Is that not so, mesdemoiselles?

MARY: No, my lord, for what love must not eventually be paid for? I'll play with you.

LORD EXRAKE: Will you, my dear? There is not so much as there once was, but come and sit on my lap.

MARY: I meant piquet, my lord. I'll sit opposite your lap.

MR MANNERS: He's not playing any more.

LORD EXRAKE: Oh, but I didn't say . . . Mr Manners, one does not refuse a lady . . . Remember that, Robert.

ROBERT: (*To* SOPHIE) Dirty old man, I can't stand him.

MR MANNERS: The gambling is serious here.

MARY: Is money ever frivolous, Mr Manners?

MR MANNERS: The stakes are high.

MARY: I can pay. Show them our money, Mrs Temptwell.

MRS TEMPTWELL: No, no, that's not necessary.

LORD EXRAKE: Indeed, mademoiselle, a beautiful young lady
can always pay, one way or another. We shall come to an
amicable arrangement.

MARY: I do not need to sell my flesh, my lord, and yours might
not fetch enough. You may choose the stakes.

LORD EXRAKE: You are blunt, mademoiselle, you remind
me . . .

ROBERT: A young woman shouldn't talk like that, it's
disgusting. Of course I blame him.

LORD EXRAKE: Ten shillings a point?

MRS TEMPTWELL: That's too high, Mary.

MARY: Shall we double it?

MR MANNERS: A pound a point. Don't play, Lord Exrake.

MARY: Are you his keeper?

MR MANNERS: I believe in keeping a sense of decency in these
proceedings.

MARY: Is risk an indecency, Mr Manners? Shall we make it five
pounds a point?

MRS TEMPTWELL: Five pounds!

LORD EXRAKE: Five pounds then.

ROBERT: That's sinful. It's my inheritance.

LORD EXRAKE: What is your name?

MARY: Mary.

MR MANNERS: Your other name?

MARY: Do you mean my patronymic? I have none. I'm
unfathered.

LORD EXRAKE: (*To* SOPHIE) And you, my pretty? Forgive me
for not noticing you before, mademoiselle. You're not as
tall as your friend, but not so fierce neither. I think I like
you better.

MARY: Her name's Sophie. Let's play.

LORD EXRAKE: Sophie . . . such a beautiful name . . . you
remind me . . .

ROBERT: (*To* SOPHIE) I've never been with a woman –
(LORD EXRAKE *and* MARY *cut the cards.*)

MARY: I am elder.

LORD EXRAKE: And I the youth. Ah, youth. It was as a mere
youth . . . have I told you, Mr Manners?

MR MANNERS: Yes, you have.
(LORD EXRAKE *deals.* MARY *exchanges five cards,* LORD
EXRAKE *three.*)

ROBERT: But I know how to write about women. I know what
women need. I don't understand why they won't listen.

LORD EXRAKE: It was the nights . . . The nights aren't the
same these days. What do you do with your nights, Mr
Manners?

MR MANNERS: I spend most of them in the Cabinet trying to
quiet the Americans. It's a most trying country.

LORD EXRAKE: We didn't have Americans in my day. The
Scots were exotic enough for us. Ah, the old world . . .
Perhaps that's what's wrong with Robert.

MARY: Point of five.

LORD EXRAKE: Making?

MARY: Forty-nine.

LORD EXRAKE: Good.

MARY: In hearts. Lord Exrake, it is my hand that should
interest you, not my legs. Keep your feet to yourself.

LORD EXRAKE: Alas, don't hobble me, mademoiselle. It was
thinking of my youth . . . where is the other one, the
beautiful Sophie? Come and sit on my lap, my dear, your
friend is too severe. That is, if your dear mama will allow.

MARY: She's not our mama, she's our duenna. Keeps the grim
suitor prudence from our hearts.

MRS TEMPTWELL: Do what you want with her, Lord Exrake,
she never resists.

SOPHIE: Mrs Temptwell, please –

ROBERT: (*To* SOPHIE) When I have my school, you'll be saved

from all this. Your work will be hard but decent and you'll
celebrate your chastity.

MR MANNERS: (*To* MARY) You ought not to be here, Mary. I
know who you are.

MARY: How can you when I do not even know myself? Do you
know yourself, Mr Manners?

MRS TEMPTWELL: Concentrate on the game, Mary.

MARY: And a quart major.

LORD EXRAKE: Good.

(*He pulls* SOPHIE *to him.*)

Do sit on my lap, belle Sophie, your friend frightens me.

MARY: You stand behind me, Mr Manners, shall I invite you on
my lap?

MR MANNERS: I want to watch you play.

MARY: A voyeur. And I took you for a man of action. That's
five for point, four for the sequence, nine.

LORD EXRAKE: No, no, do not try to escape, Sophie.

MARY: Three knaves?

LORD EXRAKE: Three knaves are not good.

MARY: Your suspicions run down my neck, Mr Manners, you
do not trust the fairness of the fair sex. I promise I've
encountered fortune head on, no female detours for me.
And one for leading, ten.

(MARY *leads to the first trick.*)

LORD EXRAKE: I count fourteen tens and three queens. You
talk too much. It is not that I mind women who talk. In
the salons, women used to talk, but in the salons, they
talked in French . . . Do you know the salons, Mr
Manners?

(*They play their tricks.*)

MR MANNERS: No. Your discards were good, Mary.

MARY: One learns. To discard. Yours too must be good.

MR MANNERS: It is more in man's nature.

MARY: Then nature is simply a matter of practice. Eleven,
twelve, thirteen, fourteen, fifteen.

LORD EXRAKE: Ah, the salons . . . Mademoiselle de
Lespinasse. I'll give you an introduction, Robert, although

now . . . she spoke to me in the strictest confidence . . . I
was much in demand then. Nineteen, twenty, twenty-one,
twenty-two, twenty-three.

MARY: Seventeen, eighteen, and ten for cards, twenty-eight.
I've won.

MR MANNERS: Well played. Your hand was weak.

MARY: Did you take me for a fool?

MR MANNERS: I don't make quick judgements.

MARY: Then you lack imagination. Second deal.
(MARY *deals*.)

MR MANNERS: No. Imagination has been one of my wisest
discards.

MARY: You are the elder, Lord Exrake.

LORD EXRAKE: Alas, I am, I am, but once . . . *l'Anglais gallant*,
they used to call me. Some wag said an *Anglais gallant* was
a contradiction in terms, but Mademoiselle de Lespinasse
. . . *Les Anglais*, she said, *ah, les Anglais*. Such phlegmatic
exteriors, but beneath *tout cela*. *Quel* fire, she said, what
feu. Les Anglais . . .
(LORD EXRAKE *has discarded hesitantly and picked up his
new cards*.)
Point of seven.

MARY: Not good.

LORD EXRAKE: I have met Italians, she said, no more than
gesture deep. Quart minor.

MARY: Not good.

LORD EXRAKE: And the Spanish, who like scorpions sting
themselves to death with their own passion. A trio of
Kings.

MARY: Not good.

EXRAKE: Ah. Mm. And the Dutch . . . The Dutch. One for the
heart, makes eight.

MARY: (*Triumphantly*) *Seizième* for sixteen, a *quatorze* of knaves,
a trio of aces, that's thirty-three and the repique, ninety-
three.

LORD EXRAKE: She had travelled. Will you travel with me,
Sophie? Your friend plays too well.

(*They play out their tricks.* LORD EXRAKE *wins one trick*, MARY *the rest.*)

MARY: That is yours.

LORD EXRAKE: It was on my travels I met Mademoiselle Sophie, or was it Sylvie? She was with that writer, what was his name? *Double entendre*, I think. But he wrote so much, and pleasure needs time. It is a demanding vocation. *A l'amour comme à la guerre*, love and war, the same, *ainsi de suite*.

MARY: No. A soldier braves death but obeys authority. The pleasure seeker braves authority but gives in to annihilation. This makes pleasure the heroism of the disobedient, whereas war is for those who dare not step out of line, or cowards. An interesting paradox, is it not, Mr Manners?

MR MANNERS: I don't like paradoxes, they give me bad dreams.

MARY: I score one hundred and fourteen.

MRS TEMPTWELL: Stop now, Mary.

MARY: Another game, Lord Exrake?

LORD EXRAKE: I too was bold when I was young. I believed I had time to waste.

(*They now play very fast.*)

MARY: I don't waste time, I love it.

LORD EXRAKE: But it isn't wasted time that's so painful, no, wasted time is time that never existed. It's the memories.

MARY: Memories are for the idle, I'll never be idle.

LORD EXRAKE: Memories . . . those leeches of the mind, exquisite moments, forever past, that now suck you dry.

MARY: I shall never have memories, I won't have time.

MR MANNERS: Everyone has memories, but they can be changed. An entire people's memory may be changed.

MRS TEMPTWELL: I live on my memories.

SOPHIE: I like mine.

ROBERT: Mine are awful. My mother was always writing pamphlets. But sometimes the present is worse.
(*He goes.*)

LORD EXRAKE: I suffer the torment of Tantalus. I want to

reach out my hand to seize those moments and live them again. Do you understand me?

MARY: I score one hundred and twenty.

LORD EXRAKE: It isn't the fear of death that keeps me here all night.

MARY: I sleep as little as I can, the world gives me such pleasure.

LORD EXRAKE: Keeps me here all night, pawing at youth, it's the fear of those memories. The moments mock me with their vanished existence. You'll see.

MARY: Why are you trying to frighten me?

LORD EXRAKE: Why shouldn't you know that age is horrible?

MARY: One hundred and seventy-two. I've lost count of the total.

MRS TEMPTWELL: Lord Exrake owes you two thousand six hundred and eighty pounds.

MARY: Another game?

LORD EXRAKE: No, no. You remind me of my youth.

MARY: But you have failed to remind me of my old age. Come, Sophie, look at all this delightful money. I could double it before dawn.

LORD EXRAKE: It was the first time I slept through the dawn that the memories took over. There were suddenly too many years between me and the new day. Do I make myself clear? They buzz in my ears and I can't hear.

(MARY *turns away.* LORD GORDON *comes on.*)

MARY: How's your cock, Lord Gordon?

LORD GORDON: Bruised from the last encounter. Do I know you?

MARY: Mine's fighting fit. Will you pit yours against mine?

LORD GORDON: I never bet against a woman.

MARY: Afraid of bad luck? Scratch a parliamentarian, you find a follower of folk tales.

SOPHIE: Mrs Temptwell, it was him.

MRS TEMPTWELL: So?

LORD GORDON: (*To* MARY) When my cock recovers, perhaps.

MARY: Cocks recover so slowly and I presume you have no
    spare?
LORD GORDON: I have seen you before.
    (MR HARDLONG *comes on. The men ignore him.*)
MARY: How can I remember a man who won't expose his cock?
    Are you looking for me, Mr Hardlong?
MR HARDLONG: No, for Sophie.
MARY: Who will fight my cock?
LORD EXRAKE: I have one.
MARY: At your age, Lord Exrake, it's still active?
LORD EXRAKE: My cock is young.
MARY: So, so, wondrous nature. Is it ready?
LORD EXRAKE: Spurred and trimmed. I've left your friend,
    she's charming but too quiet. At my age one needs a
    challenge, so I've come back to you.
MARY: I too need a challenge and I'd prefer to pit against Mr
    Hardlong's cock. Will you?
MR HARDLONG: I'll do anything if Sophie will stand by me.
MRS TEMPTWELL: Sophie does what she's told.
MR MANNERS: You ought to choose your opponents more
    carefully, Mary.
MARY: I didn't escape from propriety to fall into snobbery.
MR MANNERS: That's a mistake. Snobbery is cheap to practise
    and has saved many a nonentity.
MARY: Just so. I don't need it. Where's my whip, Mrs
    Temptwell?
MRS TEMPTWELL: Don't bet too much.
MARY: Two hundred and fifty guineas, Mr Hardlong?
    (*They touch their whips.*)
LORD EXRAKE: Ladies didn't have cocks in my day.
    (*They release the birds from the cloth sacks.*)
MARY: Now my bird, fight for me, match my courage and my
    strength.
    (*Screams and urgings from all.*)
MR MANNERS: Your cock's dead.
MARY: No, look, look. It was a ruse. My cock's risen and
    stricken Mr Hardlong's. Ha!

MR HARDLONG: My cock's failed me.

MARY: That happens, Mr Hardlong, even to the best. I keep winning, I keep winning.

MR HARDLONG: Will you come and console me, Sophie?

MARY: Mr Hardlong, it is I who have the money. Will you come to me?

MR HARDLONG: I want Sophie.

MARY: Does she want you? Sophie, come here. Here: two hundred and fifty guineas.

(*She throws her the sack of money.*)

SOPHIE: Oh, no, I can't.

MRS TEMPTWELL: Take it.

SOPHIE: Thank you, Miss Mary.

MARY: Yes, but you must work for it.

(*Pause.*)

Nothing for nothing. That's their law. When they offer you money, you know what for. Well?

SOPHIE: I don't understand.

(MARY *turns to* SOPHIE *and lifts up her skirts to her.*)

MARY: Men don't know their way around there. You will.

SOPHIE: I –

MARY: Look. Surely it's more appealing than their drooping displays? Or do you share their prejudice?

(SOPHIE *kneels to* MARY.)

What is it, gentlemen, you turn away, you feel disgust? Why don't you look and see what it's like? When you talk of sulphurous pits, deadly darkness, it's your own imagination you see. Look. It's solid, rich, gently shaped, fully coloured. The blood flows there on the way to the heart. It answers tenderness with tenderness, there is no gaping void here, only soft bumps, corners, cool convexities. Ah, Sophie, how sweet you are, I understand why they love you. Such peace. Shall we sleep?

(*Two* OLD WOMEN *shuffle on to the stage, very very slowly.*)

No – Look, over there, the spectres of passing time. I can't bear it. Wait. Mr Manners, a race? You cannot question my choice of opponent. Four thousand pounds.

MRS TEMPTWELL: That's all our money.

MR HARDLONG: (*To* SOPHIE) Let me take you away.

MR MANNERS: Set it up, Hardlong.

(*The two* OLD WOMEN *are placed side by side.*)

MR HARDLONG: Gentlemen! last chance to win your fortune in this unique event.

(*He takes the bets.*)

Mr Manners' hag is favourite.

(*All get ready.* LORD GORDON *raises his arm. The two* OLD WOMEN *stand.*)

Go! Go!

(*The two* OLD WOMEN *start to run as fast as they can, which is extremely slowly. They cough, spit, stumble, pant, covering just a few feet.*)

MRS TEMPTWELL: Four thousand pounds. We'll go hungry if she loses.

SOPHIE: We've been well fed.

MR MANNERS: Faster, faster. There's a good girl.

LORD EXRAKE: I've put money on Miss Mary's hag, her ankles look firm.

LORD GORDON: Mr Manners' hag is taking the lead. Miss Mary's hag having a little trouble.

MARY: A cane to your back if you stumble again. Pick your feet up!

MR MANNERS: Come on, girl, you can do it.

LORD GORDON: Miss Mary's hag catching up. Is she? Yes she is. No, she's just tripped.

MARY: Your hag tripped mine, Mr Manners. I saw.

LORD GORDON: No, there was no foul play. Mr Manners' hag still in the lead, and gaining.

LORD EXRAKE: Get up, girl, get up. Go.

MR HARDLONG: She's too broad in the back, bad for balance.

MR MANNERS: Faster, faster.

LORD GORDON: Miss Mary's hag a little winded. Making an effort, yes, she's closing the gap. Yes. Will she do it?

MR MANNERS: Steady, girl, steady.

LORD GORDON: Miss Mary's hag pulling ahead, yes, Mr Manners' hag slowing down.

MARY: Go on, you can do it.

SOPHIE: She's ahead, she'll win. Faster. Faster.

MRS TEMPTWELL: You're cheering yourself on. That could be us.

SOPHIE: You cheer her on.

LORD GORDON: Miss Mary's hag now well in the lead. Yes. Mr Manners' hag stumbles.
(*They cheer.*)

LORD EXRAKE: I've always been a good judge of ankles.

LORD GORDON: Only a few steps to the finishing line. It looks like Miss Mary's hag will win. But no. Look. Oh, what a jump. Look at that, what an effort and is it? Yes it is. It's Mr Manners' hag first, what a superb effort, what a close race, but it's Mr Manners' hag.
(*More cheers.*)

MARY: I saw him give her brandy.

MR MANNERS: That is not against the rules.

LORD GORDON: Mr Manners never breaks the rules. You owe him four thousand pounds.

MRS TEMPTWELL: Don't give it to him. He likes you. Burst into tears.

MARY: What? Turn female now?

MRS TEMPTWELL: (*To* SOPHIE) We go hungry for her vanity.

MARY: Here, Mr Manners. I've lost.

MR MANNERS: I have that effect on people.

LORD EXRAKE: I once lost two thousand pounds on a woodlice race. No one wants to know you when you've lost, but they forget. A few weeks in Ipswich always helps.

MR MANNERS: Where's my hag? Here's a shilling for you, you ran well.
(*The other* OLD WOMAN *approaches* MARY *who ignores her.*)

OLD WOMAN: Please, Miss.

MARY: Let's go.

OLD WOMAN: I ran for you.

MARY: And lost. Don't touch me.

OLD WOMAN: I've been ill. Be kind.

MARY: Why? Look around. Do you see kindness anywhere? Where is it?

OLD WOMAN: Give me something.

MARY: I'll give you something priceless. Have you heard of knowledge?

(*She takes the whip and beats her.*)

There is no kindness. The world is a dry place.

OLD WOMAN: Please.

MARY: What, you want more?

(*She beats her again. The* OLD WOMAN *falls.*)

Have I hurt her?

(*She bends over her.*)

I've seen her before. Or was it her sister? Why do you all stare at me? She was standing outside church. My father told me to give her some money. He gave me a coin. I gave her the coin, smiling. She smiled. I smiled more kindly. My father smiled. I followed his glance and saw a lady and a young man, her son. They were smiling. My father gave me another coin. I moved closer to her, my steps lit by everyone's smiles. I remember watching the movement of my wrist as I put the coin in her hand. I smiled at its grace. (*Pause.*) Was that better? Tell me, was that better?

INTERVAL

ACT THREE

SCENE I

Vauxhall Gardens at night. MARY *and* MRS TEMPTWELL *stand in the dark, waiting. Music and lights in the background.* MARY *has a rounded stomach under dirty clothes.*

MRS TEMPTWELL: Voices. Coming this way.
    (*They listen.*)
MARY: They've turned down another path.
MRS TEMPTWELL: They're coming closer.
MARY: They've turned away. Your hearing's blunt.
    (*They listen.*)
MRS TEMPTWELL: Footsteps on the grass.
MARY: (*Listens*) They're not his.
MRS TEMPTWELL: You can't know that. Shht.
MARY: Those footsteps bounded my happiness for eighteen
    years. I'd recognize them now. Damn. This itch.
    (*She scratches herself. Listens.*)
    Shht. No.
MRS TEMPTWELL: Are you miserable?
MARY: You're waiting for my yes, aren't you? You'll chew on
    that yes like a hungry dog, spit it up and chew again. Well,
    you can beg for your yes. Do a trick for me, Mrs
    Temptwell. Say something interesting. You know I hate
    silence. And stop smiling.
MRS TEMPTWELL: You're seeing things.
MARY: I saw your evil grin through the darkness. Cover up
    your teeth, please, they make me ill.
MRS TEMPTWELL: It's your condition. I told you to sit.
MARY: Damn this leech in my stomach, sucking at my blood,
    determined to wriggle itself into life. Why can't you do
    something about it, you old wizard?
MRS TEMPTWELL: If I was the devil we wouldn't be shivering
    in Vauxhall Gardens waiting for our supper.

MARY: I could kill the man who did this. I found him in the Haymarket, he looked strong, seemed to have some wit and the night was soft and thick. We went to Westminster Bridge, I liked that, the water rushing beneath me, cool air through my legs, until I discovered he was wearing a pigskin. New invention from Holland, he explained. He wouldn't catch my itching boils and I'd be protected from this. Fair exchange. So I had this piece of bookbinding scratching inside me and his words scratching at my intelligence. I'd mistaken talkativeness for wit. I hope he caught my infection. Footsteps. No. Why is it the one time I had no pleasure my body decided to give life? What's the meaning of that? Why don't you answer? Why do you never say anything? Has it ever happened to you? Were you ever young? Answer my questions, damn you. Who are you?

MRS TEMPTWELL: It won't interest you.

MARY: You don't know what interests me.

MRS TEMPTWELL: If you had an interest in anybody else, you wouldn't have thrown all your money away.

MARY: I was only trying to determine whether greed was the dominant worm in the human heart. I admit the experiments were costly. You didn't have to stay.

MRS TEMPTWELL: I hear something.

MARY: Let's rob the first person who comes.

MRS TEMPTWELL: Don't you want to see him? Find out how deeply he's mourning his dear dead daughter?

MARY: How easily he cancelled my existence.

MRS TEMPTWELL: He's in the Cabinet now. He's happy.

MARY: Tell me a story.

MRS TEMPTWELL: I don't know any.

MARY: Go away then. Do you enjoy this misery? Distract me, damn you. Tell me your story. Where were you born? Don't you dare not answer.

MRS TEMPTWELL: The country.

MARY: The country. The country. There are trees here.

MRS TEMPTWELL: The North.

MARY: I know that from your granite face. Where?

MRS TEMPTWELL: Don't shout or they'll hear us.

MARY: Then talk. Remember something.

MRS TEMPTWELL: I had a grandmother.

MARY: I had a father.

MRS TEMPTWELL: She was hanged as a witch.

MARY: That's better.

MRS TEMPTWELL: That's all.

MARY: Aren't there laws against hanging witches?

MRS TEMPTWELL: It depends on the magistrate.

MARY: And she taught you to cast spells?

MRS TEMPTWELL: She was an old woman, and poor. She talked to herself because she was angry and no one listened.

MARY: Tell me more. Tell me everything.

MRS TEMPTWELL: They put a nail through her tongue.

MARY: And then?

MRS TEMPTWELL: She was naked. I remember how thin she was. And the hair, the hair between her legs. It was white. That's all I remember.

MARY: Did people cry?

MRS TEMPTWELL: They laughed. I laughed too once I'd forgotten she was my grandmother. The magistrate laughed loudest. She'd been on his land and he'd taken her cottage but she stayed at his gates, wouldn't leave. She asked for justice, he heard a witch's spell.

MARY: How interesting to have so much power and still so much fear.

MRS TEMPTWELL: He also enjoyed humiliating her. Everyone did. It's an unusual experience . . .

MARY: Tell me, Mrs Temptwell, are we imitators by nature wishing to do what we see and hear? Or is every crime already in the human heart, dormant, waiting only to be tickled out?

MRS TEMPTWELL: Footsteps.

MARY: His.

(GILES *and* SOPHIE *appear. She is leading him.*)

GILES: Where are you taking me, my sweet? No need to come
this far.

SOPHIE: I'm afraid of being seen, Sir.

GILES: Let's stop at this tree.

SOPHIE: This way, Sir.

GILES: I'm in such a hurry.

MARY: Here, Sir.

GILES: Who's that?

MRS TEMPTWELL: A woman, Sir.

GILES: Sophie, where are you?

MRS TEMPTWELL: Forget Sophie, Sir, she's docile but dull.
Look here.

GILES: I can't see anything.

MARY: Here, Sir, I'll entertain you.

MRS TEMPTWELL: She's fanciful and clever and I'm practical
and knowing, if not so young.

GILES: I want a woman, not a personality. Sophie . . .

MRS TEMPTWELL: A drawbridge: the treasures are here.

MARY: Here, Sir.

MRS TEMPTWELL: Go to Mary.

GILES: Mary . . .

MRS TEMPTWELL: Lovely name, Mary, isn't it?

GILES: Sophie's young. I want someone very young.

MARY: I'm young, Sir, and know things Sophie does not know.
Don't turn away, Sir, rejection is so painful. Come here.

GILES: If it means that much to you . . . this isn't a trick?
You're not more expensive?

MRS TEMPTWELL: Labour is cheap, there's too much of it. And
it's not as good as the machines. Perhaps one day this too
will be done by machines. Would you like that, Sir?

GILES: At least machines don't talk.

MARY: But my conversation, Sir, is my greatest charm. Come.

GILES: It's so dark.

MARY: Isn't light the greatest mistake of this century? We light
the streets only to stare at dirt. As for the lantern we poke
into nature's crevasses, what has it revealed? Beauty? Or
the most terrifying chaos? And if I take a close look at

nature now, I mean your nature, what will I find?
(*As she talks, she unbuttons* GILES.)
That it's tame, Sir, most tame, but our gardeners have
taught us to make it wild, with the help of a little art.

GILES: (*Feebly*) Must you talk so much?

MARY: It's my father who taught me to talk, Sir. He didn't
suspect he'd also be teaching me to think. He was not a
sensitive man and didn't know how words crawl into the
mind and bore holes that will never again be filled. What is
a question, Sir, but a thought that itches? Some are mild,
the merest rash but some are cankerous, infectious, without
cure. Do you have children, Sir, to grace your old age?
Men often tell me I remind them of their daughters. You
look sad, Sir, is your daughter dead? Did she die of a chill?
That happens with women of graceful breeding, the blood
becomes too polite to flow through the body. As long as she
died young, men prefer that. I've heard many confessions.
One man told me he locked up his wife for seventeen years
and she still had the vulgarity not to die. Age, after all, is a
manly quality. But even manly age, it seems, needs a little
help if we're to get anywhere. A rub, will that do?
(*She begins to massage him.*)
It helps men to think of their daughters when I do this.
You didn't kill yours, did you? Ah, I see it works. We're
ready. Front or back? Oh, the bird's already flown the
cage. Happens. Must have been the thrill of my
conversation. Or thinking of your daughter.
(MARY *uncovers her face.*)
But you recognized your daughter some time ago, Papa, by
the grace of her conversation.
(*Pause.*)
How did you say your daughter died? Did you starve her
with your puny rations of approval? Immolate her to the
country's future? But she's here. Look.

GILES: I have no daughter.

MARY: My name is Mary Traverse. Your wife had little chance
of fathering me elsewhere.

GILES: You're a whore.

MARY: Is a daughter not a daughter when she's a whore? Or can she not be your daughter? Which words are at war here: whore, daughter, my? I am a daughter, but not yours, I am your whore but not your daughter. You dismiss the 'my' with such ease, you make fatherhood an act of grace, an honour I must buy with my graces, which you withdraw as soon as I disgrace you.

GILES: What do you want from me?

MARY: Two things. Look at me.

GILES: Tell me what you want.

MARY: I'm here, Papa, Here. Look at me.
    (*Pause.* GILES *looks.*)
    Good.

GILES: Why? I gave you everything.

MARY: Except experience.

GILES: You could have married a lord.

MARY: I said experience, not a pose. The world outside, all of it. This.

GILES: This! I did everything to keep you from this! I didn't live in a beautiful house like you as a child. I had to work hard. Very hard. Not just with my hands. I didn't mind that. But with people. I had to work at not being despised. I was able. I made money, started the potteries, bought land, made more money. Everything I make sells now. And I'm listened to. I wanted you to have the ease, the delights I never knew. I wanted to protect you from what I had experienced, the slights, the filth, protect you even from the knowledge I had experienced it.

MARY: It wasn't what I wanted.

GILES: Whenever I looked at you I could forget my first twenty years.

MARY: Yes, you took my future to rewrite your past. Oh father, don't you see that's worse than Saturn eating his own children?

GILES: I let you read too much, it's maddened you.

MARY: And when I try to explain you threaten me with a
    madhouse? How dare you!

GILES: I forbid you to speak to me in that manner!

MARY: You have no power over me, Papa. Your daughter's
    dead. Now for the second thing. I want money.

GILES: Here's fifteen guineas.

MARY: Money, Papa. Not its frayed edges.

GILES: It's the agreed price for a whore.

MARY: If I wanted to make money lying on my back, I would
    have married your lord, Papa.

GILES: But – you –

MARY: I learn. I do not whore.

GILES: I don't understand.

MARY: You don't try.

GILES: Why? But – if you – if you're not – we could forget –
    I'll find a way to bring you back. Some questions, it
    wouldn't matter. If you would come back . . . as you
    were . . .

MARY: As your graceful daughter?

GILES: My beautiful and witty daughter.

MARY: Open your eyes. Look at me.
    (GILES *looks. Silence.*)
    Do you want me back?
    (*Silence.*)
    The father I want cannot be the father of 'your' daughter.
    And yet, I want a father. Could you not be 'my' father?
    Could you not try?

GILES: I'll send you a little money.

MARY: I see. (*Pause.*) I want half your money.

GILES: No.

MARY: A small price to keep me dead, Papa. Your powerful
    friends are supping in these gardens. Shall I walk through
    the tables and cry you've whored your daughter? I'll be
    believed. I talk well. People love to think ill. Don't try to
    cheat me. I know how much you have, the factories, the
    shops, your share of the canal.

GILES: What's made you like this?

MARY: Experience is expensive and precise.

GILES: I can tell you one thing, Mary. At the end of all this, you'll find nothing. Nothing. I know. Goodbye.

(*He leaves.* MRS TEMPTWELL *steps out of the shadows.*)

MARY: The only time he says my name, it's to curse me. One more denial. And he can still make the world grow cold.

MRS TEMPTWELL: Did you see the humiliation on his face? I loved it.

MARY: Why?

MRS TEMPTWELL: He made his younger brother a magistrate. It was that magistrate who hanged my grandmother.

MARY: Ah.

MRS TEMPTWELL: It's not something you need understand.

MARY: I no longer understand anything.

MRS TEMPTWELL: At least you've experienced cruelty. Their cruelty.

MARY: Is that what it is?

MRS TEMPTWELL: Didn't it give you pleasure?

MARY: No. Sadness. And then, nothing. Nothing. The withering of the night. I'm cold.

SCENE 2

Vauxhall Gardens. SOPHIE *by herself. Then* JACK.

JACK: By yourself?

SOPHIE: Yes.

JACK: Always by yourself?

SOPHIE: Yes!

JACK: Want company?

SOPHIE: Yes.

JACK: No one to look after you?

SOPHIE: No.

JACK: Not here for the toffs!

SOPHIE: No!

JACK: I hate them.

SOPHIE: Yes?

JACK: Fat. We go hungry.

SOPHIE: Yes.

JACK: Hungry?

SOPHIE: Yes.

(*He gives her some bread.*)

JACK: Here. Good?

SOPHIE: Yes.

JACK: Stole it.

SOPHIE: Yes?

JACK: Dangerous. But not wrong.

SOPHIE: No.

JACK: Ever seen them work?

SOPHIE: No.

JACK: Come here.

SOPHIE: Yes.

JACK: Jack.

SOPHIE: Jack. Yes. Jack.

(*They kiss.*)

SCENE 3

Vauxhall Gardens. MR MANNERS, LORD GORDON.

MR MANNERS: The mob can be good or the mob can be bad, Lord Gordon, it depends on whether they do what you want them to do.

LORD GORDON: I could lead them, I could lead anything if I were made into a leader. It's getting there I find difficult.

MR MANNERS: Real power prefers to remain invisible.

LORD GORDON: I wouldn't mind not having the power. Just make me visible. Notorious.

MR MANNERS: What can I do? I'm no more than a servant.

LORD GORDON: You, Mr Manners? The man most feared in Parliament?

MR MANNERS: A mere servant, I assure you. I serve, however, an awesome power.

LORD GORDON: The King.

MR MANNERS: The King's only a human being, Gordon, a German one at that. No, I serve a divine power.

LORD GORDON: You don't mean God, you haven't become a Methodist?

MR MANNERS: Order, Gordon, order: the very manifestation of God in the universe. Have you studied the planets?

LORD GORDON: Can't say I have, no. I look at 'em.

MR MANNERS: Ordered movement, perfect, everything in its place, forever. That's why I like men who make machines. They understand eternal principles, as I do. As you must.

LORD GORDON: I'm good at adding.

MR MANNERS: When you ride in your carriage, you mustn't sit back and loll in your own comfort, no, you must study and love the smooth functioning of the vehicle. And if a wheel falls off, you must take it as a personal affront. Do you understand?

LORD GORDON: Check the wheels of my carriage . . .

MR MANNERS: So with the country. Our duty is to watch that no wheel falls off.

LORD GORDON: Do we wear splendid livery?

MR MANNERS: What?

LORD GORDON: I would like to serve the country.

MR MANNERS: Good.

LORD GORDON: When can I start?

MR MANNERS: We must wait. The times are restless.

LORD GORDON: (*Triumphantly*) The roads are bumpy!

MR MANNERS: And dangerous.

LORD GORDON: Highwaymen lurking behind every tree!

MR MANNERS: I think we've exhausted that, Gordon. It is clear we must find something new, and entertaining to the people.

LORD GORDON: Me!

MR MANNERS: Who knows? Someone . . . inevitably appears,

usually thrown up by the mob itself. And then one must be
vigilant . . . persuasive . . .

LORD GORDON: Be good to have me. Keep them quiet.

MR MANNERS: Who?

LORD GORDON: The families, you know, my uncle. The other
old families.

MR MANNERS: What do they say?

LORD GORDON: That they wouldn't invite you to their house.
Have to invite me. I'm a relative.

MR MANNERS: What else do they say?

LORD GORDON: Nothing much. Used to rule England, time to
rule again, better at it, born to it, look at the mess, all that.
I don't listen.

MR MANNERS: In times such as these, Lord Gordon, many
different people make claims for themselves. The good
servant must look for what fits best into the order of things.
It is not always obvious. It can even be surprising.

LORD GORDON: I'm here, Mr Manners, as soon as you want a
change.

MR MANNERS: No, no, Gordon, you haven't understood:
whatever happens, nothing must change.

SCENE 4

Elegant lodgings. MARY *and* SOPHIE, *well dressed, sit in silence.*

MARY: I'm cold.

SOPHIE: Are you ill, Miss Mary?

MARY: In which part of the anatomy does sadness sit, do you
know, Sophie? It's not in the heart because the heart's a
machine. So tell me how in this perfectly ordered universe
you explain the chaos of the human soul. My father's right.
I'm too clever. The inside of my skin hurts.

SOPHIE: Here's Mrs Temptwell with your milk.

(MRS TEMPTWELL *comes on.*)

MARY: Take it from her and tell her to go.

MRS TEMPTWELL: Mary –

MARY: Make her go, Sophie.

MRS TEMPTWELL: Mary –

SOPHIE: Mary wants you to go, Mrs Temptwell. Go away.
    (MRS TEMPTWELL *leaves. Silence.*)

MARY: How's your child?

SOPHIE: He died.

MARY: Did he? I didn't know. (*Pause.*) I'm sorry. (*Pause.*) Am
    I? Are you? (*Pause.*) You can have mine.

SOPHIE: Oh yes, Miss Mary, I'd like that. Please.

MARY: Why?

SOPHIE: Why what?

MARY: No. I don't want to know why. What's that noise?

SOPHIE: Shouting. The price of white bread has gone up again.

MARY: I thought you people ate brown bread.

SOPHIE: We don't like it. My teeth aren't strong enough to eat
    brown bread. The merchants are hiding sacks of flour to
    make the prices go up so the people have decided to find
    the sacks and take them by force. Then they'll buy the
    sacks at a fair price. Jack says it's happening all over the
    country. They've beaten some merchants.

MARY: Would you do that if you were hungry?

SOPHIE: Oh no.

MARY: If you were very hungry? I would. But I don't have to.
    Do you ever think about that?

SOPHIE: About what?

MARY: Come here. Closer. We're the same age. Why do you
    never look at me? (*Pause.*) Look into my eyes.

SOPHIE: They're very beautiful, Miss Mary.

MARY: What do you think of me?

SOPHIE: You're feverish, Miss Mary. I'll bring you a brandy.

MARY: I asked you a question. What do you think of me?

SOPHIE: I don't understand.

MARY: You have a mind. Tell me what it sees.

SOPHIE: The country, Miss Mary. Fields. The fields I used to
    walk in as a child. That's what it sees. Green.

MARY: What questions does it ask?

THE GRACE OF MARY TRAVERSE

SOPHIE: Questions? Yes. How can I be less tired? Why does my belly hurt? Is that what you call thinking? And how good white bread is. Sometimes I think about the baby, but not much.

MARY: What do you think about my life?

SOPHIE: I hope it will be a long one.

MARY: Are you pretending to be stupid?

SOPHIE: I don't understand, Miss Mary. (*Pause.*) I feel things.

MARY: What do you feel for me? Hatred? Contempt? Don't be afraid, Sophie, answer.

SOPHIE: I don't feel – that way. I feel the cold. And the heat even more than the cold.

MARY: Sophie!

SOPHIE: I don't have time to think the way you do. Please, Miss Mary, let me get you some wine.

MARY: Do I disgust you?

SOPHIE: You found me on the streets. I had nothing.

MARY: I pushed you on the streets as well. You took my place with Lord Gordon. What did you feel then? What did you feel in the gambling den, servicing my pleasures? What did you feel?

SOPHIE: I don't know. I can't remember. Sometimes I don't feel I'm there. It could be someone else. And I'm walking in the fields. So I don't mind much. My brother used to touch me. He was strong and I learned to make it not me. I was somewhere else. But when I want to, with Jack, I'm there. And then not. It's not difficult.

MARY: I see. I'm not sorry then. Perhaps I never was. Tell Mrs Temptwell to come to me with some ideas.

(MRS TEMPTWELL *comes on immediately*.)

MRS TEMPTWELL: I knew our quiet Sophie wouldn't entertain you long. You can go, Sophie.

MARY: No, let her stay.

(*Pause.*)

Well?

MRS TEMPTWELL: I've seen some beautiful jewels we could acquire.

MARY: Jewels.

MRS TEMPTWELL: There are women wrestling in Clerkenwell. You like that.

MARY: Do I?

(Silence.)

Will I have to kill myself to make the time pass? Something. Something. And I can't sleep. Do you have dreams, Sophie?

SOPHIE: I dream of a little cottage . . .

MARY: Oh stop.

MRS TEMPTWELL: Why don't you go, Sophie?

SOPHIE: Jack dreams of a new world.

MARY: A new world? Does he? A new world . . . who's Jack?

SOPHIE: He's – Jack. He's very handsome.

MARY: All men are handsome when we drape them with our longings. A new world . . . even Sophie's Jack has more interesting thoughts than I do. Why?

MRS TEMPTWELL: We'll think of something tomorrow.

MARY: Another endless round of puny, private vice? This isn't experience, Mrs Temptwell, this is another bounded room. You promised more, remember? They must have more than this. What? Yes . . . they go to war. They go to war . . .

MRS TEMPTWELL: We could go to America.

MARY: Or they dream of new worlds. They let their imaginations roam freely over the future, yes, they think about the country, and then they rule the country. What sort of a new world does Jack dream of, Sophie? Who is Jack?

SCENE 5

A cobbler's basement in Southwark. JACK, *then* MARY, SOPHIE, MRS TEMPTWELL.

JACK: A travelling preacher taught me how to read. I was sixteen. He wanted me to spread the word of God. But I

didn't like the word of God. Fear and obedience.
Obedience and fear. I heard another word. Freedom. The
preacher said God would punish me for such devilish
rebellion. And he did. I can't talk. I want to tell people
about freedom. I can't explain it. I have other words:
equality, justice, right, but they're rough stones that won't
stand together to make a house. I have a new world, in my
head, I can't make it come out, I can't give it to anyone. I
look across the river at those houses of tyrants, I know the
world needs me, but I'm cursed. Silent.

MARY: I can talk, Jack, but until now I had nothing to say. I
understand what it is to need freedom. I thought it was
something only I wanted, but now I know it is a longing in
every human heart. I have watched freedom, beautiful
freedom, hunted from every street and I know what it is to
bang at the doors of tyranny. I could speak for you, Jack, if
you taught me what to say.

JACK: You?

MARY: Why not?

SOPHIE: She can help us, Jack.

JACK: You wouldn't understand about equality.

MARY: I know the humiliation of being denied equality, Jack,
and that it is a dignity due to all, men and women, rich and
poor.

JACK: There should be no poor. Government makes people
poor. Do you understand about natural rights?

MARY: I used to talk about nature.

JACK: Everyone is born with them. Born.

MARY: Yes: Nature has given us certain unquestionable,
inalienable rights but these have been taken from us by
those who set themselves above us.

JACK: We have to get them back.

MARY: Wrench back from an usurping, base and selfish
government what is ours by right.

JACK: And the new world – the new world –

MARY: Will be a world ruled by us, for our delight, a world of

hope for all. Oh Jack, that's beautiful. Let's go tell
everyone.

JACK: The tyrants: show them up.

MARY: We'll explain to the people that they worship an
authority that mocks, abuses and eventually kills them.

JACK: That's it, Mary.

MARY: Let's go, let's go quickly.

MRS TEMPTWELL: Where are you going?

MARY: There, where the power sits. Parliament.

MRS TEMPTWELL: You're mad.

MARY: If you wish to talk like my father, go home.

MRS TEMPTWELL: She only wants power, Jack.

SOPHIE: No, she wants our good.

MARY: In the new world, they will be identical. Let's go.

SCENE 6

In front of the Houses of Parliament. JACK *and* MARY *try to get by
the* GUARD. *A* SPY *in dark clothes comes on during the
exchange, then two* OLD WOMEN, *then the* LOCKSMITH, *then*
GILES.

JACK: Listen to her.

GUARD: I told you: no petticoats in the Houses of Parliament.

MARY: I'll unpetticoat myself if it's my underwear you object
to. What I have to say is without frills.

JACK: We have the right to be heard.

GUARD: I know you: you're the one who keeps bringing
petitions.

MARY: No petticoats, no petitions, what do you allow in that
house which is supposed to represent us all?

JACK: Thieves and hangmen. Let the working man in.

SPY: (*To an* OLD WOMAN) Do you know that woman?

MARY: We'll change history if we go in there. Don't you want a
change?

GUARD: No.

MARY: Wouldn't you like a world where everyone was free to choose their future?

GUARD: Not much.

MARY: Oh the precious maidenhead of a young man. No virgin shuts her legs as tight as you your mind. No new thought will penetrate to make you bleed.

GUARD: Watch your language, Miss.

MARY: What are they doing for you in there? What?

JACK: Nothing, that's what.

SPY: (*To the* OLD WOMAN) Has she ever spoken here before?

GUARD: And what would your world do for me, eh?

MARY: It would do what you asked because it would be a world you would have made. What have those in there done to deserve their power? Nothing.

JACK: They stole it from us, that's what.

SPY: (*To the* OLD WOMAN) You don't know her name, do you?

MARY: Our sons and daughters will share the land.

OLD WOMAN: I'm not giving anything to my daughter. She's a whore.

MARY: In the new world, there will be no whores, there won't have to be.

LOCKSMITH: If I want a whore and I can pay for her, I have a right to that whore.

MARY: No one has the right to pleasure at the cost of another's pain. In the new world, everyone will have their natural, just, share of pleasure. Think of a world where there is no hoarding of ill-begotten riches, no more theft –

LOCKSMITH: What happens to the locksmiths?

MARY: A world where there are no longer any families living in greed –

LOCKSMITH: I'm a locksmith. What good are locks without thieves?

MARY: You will make keys for all of us.

LOCKSMITH: Oh. No. You get paid more for locks than keys.

JACK: The working man pays for everything and gets nothing.

MARY: Do you know how much our King costs us?

SPY: This is sedition.

MARY: Eight hundred thousand pounds sterling a year.

SPY: (*To the* OLD WOMAN) Remember what she says, will you. (*The* SPY *leaves quickly.*)

MARY: How much bread does eight hundred thousand pounds a year buy?

OLD WOMAN: I saw the King the other day. He looks ever such a gentleman.

LOCKSMITH: Why don't you go to America if you don't like it here? They make you pick cotton in the heat there and you die in two weeks.

MARY: Who was the first King of England? A French bandit.

OLD WOMAN: I didn't know that. Is that why he speaks so different from us?

JACK: A King's privilege is an insult to the working people.

MARY: What does the King do for us?

LOCKSMITH: If that was my daughter, I'd have her locked up.

GILES: Why? She speaks well. What she says is wrong, of course.

MARY: Let us share in the building of a new world.

JACK: All men will be brothers.

MARY: A world that is gentle, wise, free, uncircumscribed.

GILES: I used to have dreams like that.

MARY: Imagine how you would run this world and now, ask yourselves this: why have we no bread to eat?

OLD WOMAN: I've asked that before. No one tells me.

MARY: Ask yourselves why our children are born to hunger and toil.

OLD WOMAN: Why?

(MR MANNERS *comes on from the Houses of Parliament.*)

MARY: Ask yourselves why they are indifferent to our needs.

OLD WOMAN/LOCKSMITH: Why?

MARY: Ask yourselves why they won't let us speak out.

ALL: Why?

MR MANNERS: Why do you say all this out here and not in there?

MARY/ALL: Yes. Why?

THE GRACE OF MARY TRAVERSE

MR MANNERS: They'd like to have you in there. They are interested in what you have to say.

JACK: They don't let the people in there.

MR MANNERS: That can change.

MARY: You'll let us into the House?

MR MANNERS: Not the House exactly, but there are many rooms.

MARY: Let's go.

MR MANNERS: Just you – for the moment.

JACK: Go in, Mary. Talk to them about the people.

MARY: I'll see what they have to say and come back.

(MARY and MR MANNERS leave.)

GUARD: She was better out here.

GILES: People were listening to her. She made them listen.

JACK: She'll talk to them and come back.

GUARD: I've seen people go in there and come out very different.

JACK: Even they will have to listen to common sense.

GUARD: Are you going to this new world?

LOCKSMITH: I'm not having a world without locks.

SCENE 7

Preparations for a midnight conversation. MRS TEMPTWELL *and* SOPHIE *set out the chairs.*

MRS TEMPTWELL: We must stop her.

SOPHIE: Why? She's so gay.

MRS TEMPTWELL: And us?

SOPHIE: She said I could go to the country and look after her child.

MRS TEMPTWELL: No!

SOPHIE: Please don't stop me from having the child.

MRS TEMPTWELL: She had you raped, she made you whore, she caused the misery that killed your child and now you'll slave to bring up her reject?

SOPHIE: She said we could have a cottage.

MRS TEMPTWELL: Until she takes it to make way for some roses. Don't you know what they're like?

SOPHIE: Who?

MRS TEMPTWELL: Listen to these words, Sophie: freeborn Englishman. Aren't they sweet?

SOPHIE: I suppose so.

MRS TEMPTWELL: My father was a freeborn Englishman. So was yours.

SOPHIE: I never knew him.

MRS TEMPTWELL: But us? I'm a servant. Nothing my own, no small piece of ground, no hour, no sleep she can't break with a bell. Do you understand, girl?

SOPHIE: Did you suffer misfortune?

MRS TEMPTWELL: He was our misfortune, her father. I had to watch my mother grow thin as hunger and die. I curse the whole family.

SOPHIE: You could get another place.

MRS TEMPTWELL: She'll be as low as us when I'm finished. And you could help, Sophie.

SOPHIE: I don't feel low.

MRS TEMPTWELL: When you know all I know, you'll be angry too.

SOPHIE: When I've been angry, it's only made it all worse. No, I won't be angry. Is that all the chairs?

MRS TEMPTWELL: We could work together. I'll be your friend.

SOPHIE: You said that when you brought me into the house.

MRS TEMPTWELL: I didn't know how vicious she was. And now she'll do us even more harm with these ideas of hers.

SOPHIE: I like it when she speaks of the new world. So does Jack.

MRS TEMPTWELL: New world? This is no way to get rid of the old.

SCENE 8

A midnight conversation: the last stages of a drunken dinner.
SOPHIE, MRS TEMPTWELL, MARY, MR MANNERS, JACK, *the*
GUARD, LORD GORDON.

MARY: Sophie, more wine for the gentlemen and for me.
MR MANNERS: No more for me.
MARY: Moderation in all things, Mr Manners?
MR MANNERS: Historical moments need level heads.
MARY: Why? The future is intoxicating.
JACK: I'm a working man. I drink gin.
MRS TEMPTWELL: And gin for me.
MARY: I forgot you, Mrs Temptwell.
MRS TEMPTWELL: That's what happens to working people,
  Jack.
GUARD: It's all going to change now.
MRS TEMPTWELL: Is it?
MARY: I have asked you all here this evening that we may
  hammer out our common cause. Mr Manners tells me it's a
  good time to be heard.
JACK: We want bread. Bread for everyone.
MARY: We have to ask for more than bread.
JACK: Every man has a right to eat.
MARY: It's a right remembered only by the hungry. No, we
  need something big enough to net the future.
JACK: All men are born equal.
MR MANNERS: Too general. We don't listen to abstractions in
  England.
MARY: But we do need a good cry as our banner. I remember
  my father talking about the frenzy caused by the cry
  Wilkes and Liberty.
LORD GORDON: What about Silks and Tyranny? (*Pause.*) Milk
  and Bigotry?
  (*Silence.*)
  There's a Wilkes in the House. Tory chap isn't he?

MR MANNERS: He's calmed down since the sixties. The House does that.

JACK: Liberty. We'd go for that.

MARY: Yes. Liberty is a beautiful word.

MR MANNERS: Dangerous, Mary.

GUARD: Will there be liberty in the new world?

MARY: Oh yes. (*To* MR MANNERS) Why dangerous? It's what we want.

MR MANNERS: It's been heard before and no one understands it. People were shouting for Wilkes, not for liberty.

LORD GORDON: Gordon . . . What about Gordon and Drollery? I do so wish to hear my name shouted.

MARY: Let us start again: to build a new world, one must know what is wrong with the old. What do you most want to be rid of, Jack?

JACK: Tyranny. I want to kill the tyrants.

MR MANNERS: That won't do, Mary.

MARY: Shouldn't we hear the people?

MR MANNERS: One must interpret to lead.

LORD GORDON: You said I could be the leader in this, Mr Manners, you said I could make myself known in history.

MR MANNERS: You will, Lord Gordon.

LORD GORDON: I know: the French!

MARY: What about the French?

LORD GORDON: What I most want to be rid of. Hate them. Riot against them. No French!

MR MANNERS: That's called war and we already have one.

MARY: Sophie, what do you most dislike?

SOPHIE: Me? I don't know. Bad smells.

JACK: That's my sweet lass.

LORD GORDON: Told you it was the French. No French food. That'll rouse 'em.

MR MANNERS: (*To* MARY) There's actually a clue in all that.

MARY: Where? We're not getting anywhere.

MR MANNERS: What makes a smell good or bad?

LORD GORDON: I don't know, but I know it when I smell it.

GUARD: What do smells have to do with the new world?

MRS TEMPTWELL: There won't be a new world.

JACK: I don't understand any of this. I want to organize for bread and liberty.

MRS TEMPTWELL: Go quickly before it's too late.

SOPHIE: No, Jack. Mary will help us. She's thinking for us.

MARY: Listen: our lives ought by nature to be pleasant and free, but are not. Why? We have been invaded by unnatural practices and beliefs: the bad smells. What are they?

MR MANNERS: Or: who are they?

MARY: Yes.

MR MANNERS: The Dutch . . . but one could hardly get emotional about the Dutch. The Jews . . . not enough of them. The Irish . . .

JACK: I hate the Irish, they take lower wages.

MRS TEMPTWELL: They work, like you. They're turning you against your own kind.

MARY: We must not turn against working people. What do all foreigners have in common?

LORD GORDON: They're not English.

MR MANNERS: And not Church of England.

JACK: We hate the Church.

MARY: Yes. Anything that encourages superstition, hierarchy and prejudice is vile.

MR MANNERS: That's not the Church of England. After all, the Church of England is more England than Church. The superstitions are unfortunate remains from former times . . . when we were under the Catholics. Yes. The Catholics . . .

LORD GORDON: I'm to lead a mob of Catholics?

MR MANNERS: You can't lead any mob, Gordon, you're in Parliament, remember? But you can present petitions . . .

MARY: We've done all that. We're wasting time.

MR MANNERS: Did you know there's a bill about to be presented to the House which will give back to all Catholics their right to own property? There's already fear it will cause trouble. After all, the more the Catholics take, the less for people like Jack.

MARY: What do you think of Catholics, Jack?

JACK: I don't know much. They do smoky things on Sundays and come out smelling funny.

MR MANNERS: It's much worse than that, isn't it, Mary?

MARY: Is it?

MR MANNERS: Tell Jack about the Catholics. Tell him how they stuff themselves with white bread on Sundays.

MARY: Ah, yes. They buy it all up and hoard it in their chapels, that's why there's none left for you. Mr Manners –

MR MANNERS: Tell Jack about the Pope.

MARY: He is the tyrant of tyrants –

MR MANNERS: The Pope has stores of bread in his palaces. He ships the bread secretly from England. He delights in eating Protestant bread. He would like to eat Protestants.

MARY: He makes them starve instead. Every day the number of hungry Protestants is read out to him and it makes him laugh.

JACK: Where is this Pope? I'll kill him.

MARY: All Catholics are the Pope's slaves. If he tells them to drink the blood of Protestant children with their wine, they do.

MR MANNERS: Protestant children have been known to disappear near Catholic chapels.

SOPHIE: Help!

MARY: It's the Catholics who've enclosed all the common land so they could build their chapels underground.

MRS TEMPTWELL: Oh!

MR MANNERS: That's right, Mary.

MARY: The Pope builds his palaces of luxury and depravity with the bones of murdered Protestants.

MR MANNERS: Actually, the Pope is a woman. Her red robe is dyed anew every year in putrid blood.

LORD GORDON: That's disgusting.

MARY: The Pope washes his hands in the blood of tortured Protestant babes and drinks the tears of English mothers.

SOPHIE: Mothers against the Pope!

MR MANNERS: That's not quite right.

MARY: Popery is the beast who claws at our freedom.

JACK: No to Popery, yes to Liberty.

MR MANNERS: Excellent. I suggest we leave out liberty for the moment.

LORD GORDON: No Popery! Follow me.

MR MANNERS: You, Lord Gordon, must present a petition to Parliament. It will be for the repeal of the Catholic Relief Act.

LORD GORDON: How do you spell Relief?

MARY: You'll say the people don't want Catholics back in power. We'll explain all that later, but now we must rouse the people. Stop English babies from being roasted. No Popery!

SOPHIE: Save the children. No Hopery.

MARY: No. It's no Popery.

JACK: Save the working man. No Popery!

GUARD: This new world . . .

MARY: Later, later. No Poverty. No Popery!

MRS TEMPTWELL: No fences. No Popery!

ALL: No Popery!

(*They knock over the chairs. They chant.*)

NO POPERY. NO POPERY. NO POPERY.

SCENE 9

The streets of London. MARY, MR MANNERS, LORD GORDON.

MARY: There are at least sixty thousand.

MR MANNERS: Assembling in Lambeth.

MARY: A headless snake winding its way towards Westminster Bridge. I'm breathless.

LORD GORDON: I'm a little nervous too.

MARY: It's time for you to go, Lord Gordon.

MR MANNERS: Do you have the petition ready?

LORD GORDON: Here. In my hand. Both hands.

MR MANNERS: Present it at half past two. Parliament is certain to delay any consideration of such a petition. Announce this to the crowd.

MARY: Tell them Parliament is on the side of the Catholics.

LORD GORDON: There are so many. I won't be hurt, will I?

MARY: Hurry, Lord Gordon, they're moving fast.

LORD GORDON: I never liked crowds.

MARY: Once they've surrounded Parliament, you won't get through.

LORD GORDON: It's not an easy thing to become a historical figure.

(*He leaves.*)

MARY: Thousands and I've roused them. Oh, this is a delight beyond anything. Aren't you enjoying yourself?

MR MANNERS: No. I like quiet. I'll be happy when it's over.

MARY: But this is a beginning. A new surge, which I shall lead.

MR MANNERS: To what?

MARY: Freedom.

MR MANNERS: You could be very useful, Mary, but you have a lot to learn. Power, however, is a brilliant master. Ah, listen. Shouts. The crowd's beginning to be unruly. It usually takes an hour or two, a few well-placed rumours . . .

(SOPHIE *and* JACK *run on.*)

SOPHIE: Parliament won't save us from the Catholics.

JACK: We'll save ourselves from the Catholics.

SOPHIE: We went to Duke Street.

JACK: Where there are many Catholics.

SOPHIE: We found the chapel of the ambassador from Gardenia.

MARY: Gardenia?

SOPHIE: It's a Poperist island, they capture ships and make shoes from the bones of sailors. They speak horrible spells in ill-Latin.

MARY: Sardinia!

JACK: No Popery and wooden shoes! We burnt the chapel.

SOPHIE: No Popery!

JACK: We're looking for the Bavarian chapel.

SOPHIE: Burn it! No Popery!

BOTH: No Popery!

(*They go off.*)

MARY: Let's go. Let's go and lead them.

MR MANNERS: Power always moves from behind. Let the bodies move forward.

MARY: I'm drunk with what I've done: glory!

(The GUARD *runs on. Increasing noise of riot in the background.*)

GUARD: We're thousands but act like one. We have the strength to build the new world. Yes, we'll have all we want, we'll share it, we're one.

MARY: Yes, Yes. And it's by my command. I've done it all.

(JACK *and* SOPHIE *come on.*)

JACK: The Bavarian embassy: burnt. On to Wapping. Find the Catholic houses and throw all the contents on to the street. Burn, burn it all. There's a house belongs to a Protestant manufacturer, we're going to leave it, but someone shouts: why? Catholic or not, why should anyone be possessed of more than a thousand pounds a year? Yes. Why? Burn it to the ground.

SOPHIE: No Popery. Freedom for all. Set the Protestant prisoners free. To Newgate.

JACK: To Bridewell.

BOTH: No Popery. To Clerkenwell.

(*They rush off.*)

MARY: This burning makes me a little uneasy, Mr Manners.

MR MANNERS: If you want to chop wood, you must expect the chips to fly. Are you afraid?

MARY: No indeed.

MR MANNERS: It has never been possible to define freedom.

MARY: What?

MR MANNERS: Nothing. It's getting dark. Shapes lose their firmness.

(JACK *comes on, followed by* SOPHIE. *Noise and fire in the background.*)

SOPHIE: Lord Gordon has presented the petition five times and Parliament has refused to consider it five times. And now they want to go home and sleep. We're rough handling the ones we catch. They're afraid to come out.

JACK: We're collecting for the poor mob. Give to the poor mob. For the poor mob.

SOPHIE: Here. Here's a penny for the poor mob. But I am the poor mob.

(*The* GUARD *runs on.*)

GUARD: No Popery and wooden shoes. To Holborn.

JACK: To Holborn!

SOPHIE: To Holborn!

(*They run off.*)

MARY: Why Holborn?

MR MANNERS: Streets and streets of distilleries. And they all belong to Catholics – or so the rumour goes.

MARY: I don't understand. I feel so powerful I can't think any more. Look. Fire.

MR MANNERS: There are twenty thousand gallons of gin in Holborn.

MARY: Oh God!

MR MANNERS: God?

(*Silence.* MRS TEMPTWELL *comes on slowly, charred. She speaks coldly and quietly to* MARY.)

MRS TEMPTWELL: It was dark, only a few thousand of us left. Prisoners, enthusiasts, those who couldn't free themselves from the throe of the crowd. We heard 'to Holborn'. We moved, step by step, pushed, pushing. Torches were at the front. We heard there was gin inside the houses, gin to refresh the poor mob. We rushed in, we fell in, pressed against the houses, torches high. I was pushed, I dropped, on my knees, drank the liquid, warm, then burning, looked up to see all coated in flames, fire rippling along the gin, houses, people, clothes, all burning.

(*Pause.*)

Bodies pushed each other into the burning river, slid, still trying to drink, lapped at the fire. Women, children, tearing off their clothes, people laughed. Laughed. A man next to me found a girl, rolled her into the fire, pulled up her skirts. A wall crumbled over them.

MARY: Stop.

MRS TEMPTWELL: Arms, arms waved underneath bodies. Faces, shouting, mouths black, teeth chattering: dogs snapping at the edge of hell. A woman grabbed me. 'I was just looking,' she said, 'why me?' Her cindered scalp peeled off.

MARY: Stop it!

MRS TEMPTWELL: The smell. It was the smell. I fainted, slept. All quiet, the fire on to other houses. Moved a leg, shoved a body off me, crawled on cushion of corpses, soft, nothing much left.

MARY: It's not true. It didn't happen.

(MRS TEMPTWELL *opens a bundle she's been carrying, ashes and bones, and throws them over* MARY.)

MRS TEMPTWELL: Look carefully through the teeth and you'll find some gold.

MARY: No! No! It cannot have happened.

(JACK *runs on, his clothes are smouldering.*)

JACK: Water. I'm burning. Gin. The working man's in flames. Help me.

(SOPHIE *rushes to him.*)

SOPHIE: Jack! Jack (*She laughs, drunk.*) We've burnt everything. No Popery. No nothing. Jack. Damn them. Damn everything. Jack!

(*She punches him, laughing. They fall over and roll off, together.*)

MARY: Oh my sweet Sophie. No.

(*The* GUARD *comes on.*)

GUARD: Where's my new world, where is it? Where?

(*He leaves.* GILES TRAVERSE *comes on.*)

GILES: They're moving towards the Bank of England, Mr Manners.

MR MANNERS: Ah. That must be stopped.

GILES: (*To* MARY) So you've been involved in this horror?

MARY: I didn't want it to be like this. Please believe me. I
wanted something good. I had dreams.

GILES: I could have told you how quickly private dreams
become public nightmares.

MARY: Why didn't you warn me?

GILES: Would you have listened?

MARY: Help me.

GILES: How can I, Mary? You're accountable now.

MR MANNERS: Tell them to send the soldiers, Giles. And for
the soldiers to shoot.

MARY: No!

GILES: You can't do that, Mr Manners.

MR MANNERS: If you don't agree with our policies, Giles, you
need not stay with us.

GILES: This isn't policy, this is crime.

MR MANNERS: Do what I ask or you will be suspected of
condoning this horror and encouraging these criminals.

MARY: This isn't what I wanted!

GILES: Do we ever know what we want?
(*He leaves.*)

MARY: Don't let them shoot, don't.

MR MANNERS: There is nothing so cleansing as massive death,
Mary. People return with relief to their private little pains
and stop barking at the future. It's what they want. This
will last forty years at least, forty years of rule and order.

MARY: Damn your order and your rules.

MR MANNERS: Don't damn the rules, Mary. Rules keep you
from horror and emptiness. They bring peace to the heart,
they're clear and simple, they hide the lengthening
shadows. I'll do anything to keep the rules safe, not only
for myself, but for the good of the world. One day all men
will understand the beauty of rules.
(LORD GORDON *rushes on.*)

LORD GORDON: They say it's my fault. They want to arrest me.
Save me.

MR MANNERS: We will. Give us time. Go to them now.

LORD GORDON: (*To* MARY) I've just remembered where I saw

you. I didn't mean to, that is, I didn't know – it didn't seem to matter. They're coming for me. It was better to be nobody.

(LORD GORDON *runs off. The shooting starts.*)

MARY: Please, please tell me it isn't so.

(*She screams. The shooting continues.*)

MRS TEMPTWELL: (*She has been piling the bones into a neat little pile*) One, two, twelve, one hundred, two hundred and forty thousand, three million, six million, twenty million, thirty-eight, two, eighteen, one, four, one.

MARY: Please tell me it did not happen.

ACT FOUR

SCENE I

Lodgings on Oxford Street, near Tyburn. SOPHIE *has a baby in her arms.* MRS TEMPTWELL *tries to get near her.*

SOPHIE: I love her.

MRS TEMPTWELL: That's a title to nothing. Give her to me.

SOPHIE: I've looked after her well.

MRS TEMPTWELL: You always were a fool.

SOPHIE: I want to see Miss Mary.

MRS TEMPTWELL: Do as you're told.
    (MARY *comes on. She's half-dressed, a mess. She drags herself to a chair and collapses.*)

MARY: Find a shoe for my right foot, Mrs Temptwell.

MRS TEMPTWELL: I don't know where they are.
    (MARY *kicks off her one shoe.*)

MARY: There. Order. No.
    (*She stares vacantly at one of her legs, then rolls down her one stocking. She stops.*)
    Leave it. (*To* SOPHIE) What are you doing here?

SOPHIE: You wanted to see your child.

MARY: Did I?

MRS TEMPTWELL: The future citizen of the new world.

MARY: Stop. Yes. The last act.

SOPHIE: Let me take her back to the country. We're very happy. Jack is coming soon.

MARY: Jack.

SOPHIE: They'll let him go, he didn't do anything.

MRS TEMPTWELL: You don't have to do anything to get yourself killed. Give us the child.

SOPHIE: Why?

MARY: Don't use that fateful word. Has that woman tempted you as well? Run.

MRS TEMPTWELL: You did what you wanted.

MARY: Did I? I wanted knowledge, but I didn't know what it

was. Even God wouldn't love this world if he existed, and I
know he doesn't because Voltaire said so and Voltaire is a
wit and the truth can only be funny. (*To* SOPHIE) You
never laugh.

SOPHIE: What will you do with her?

MARY: Look at us – crumbling. Too charred to scavenge for
more hope. Soon we can stop breathing – last intake of the
future. But it's not enough: our death won't redeem what's
been. I am human. I know the world. I've shared its acts.
And I would like to pour poison down the throat of this
world, burn out its hideous memories. A white cloud to
cancel it all. How? I don't know. But I can start here. I can
look after what I've generated. Stop it.

SOPHIE: You want to poison your daughter.

MRS TEMPTWELL: We're all poisoned anyway.

SOPHIE: You can't do that.

MARY: Is there anything of which we are not capable?

SOPHIE: You don't know.

MRS TEMPTWELL: She knows everything.

SOPHIE: You're wrong. You don't know how to think, Mary.
You think at a distance – too ahead or far back. If you just
looked, from near.

MRS TEMPTWELL: Our Sophie's found her tongue.

MARY: Just when I want silence.

MRS TEMPTWELL: Must be that country air. Pink cheeks. Pink
thoughts.

SOPHIE: Stop, Mrs Temptwell, don't you dare. Listen to me,
Mary. I know – about mornings.

MARY: The mornings?

SOPHIE: The first light of the morning. It's fresh, new. And I
feel a kind of hunger in the mornings, but without the
pain. Cold water on the skin. It makes her laugh too.
Think about the mornings.

MRS TEMPTWELL: Corpses look very fresh in the morning. You
can go.

SOPHIE: In London too, the windows, the crisscross of the
panes. You walk and then suddenly you're in one of the

new squares, light. Don't you understand?

MRS TEMPTWELL: We don't need an upstart bumpkin preaching to us. Go.

SOPHIE: I will not. Miss Mary is unhappy about the world, but you, Mrs Temptwell, are only full of hate. She hates you, Mary, she always did. (*Pause.*) She only wants to hurt you. Then she'll be happy.

MARY: Is that true?

(*Pause.*)

I suppose it's fair.

SOPHIE: No. It's wrong.

MARY: Not wrong, but small. As small as everything else. The world is made up of small particles of unspeakable ugliness. Why should I have the arrogance to claim a shared despair? (*To* MRS TEMPTWELL) Couldn't you have just strangled me in my cradle?

MRS TEMPTWELL: I hate you, Mary, I hate your father, I hate your child, but she's wrong, it's no longer for what you did to me, no, it's for what you are. I know who you are, now, your kind. You're the evil spirits of this world, you keep us bound. Everything you touch goes wrong, but you always save yourselves and then go all poetic over other people's bodies. I know all we need is your death and then it won't go wrong again. Then there can be a new world. I'm starting here, but we'll get all of you.

MARY: More burning, more bones.

MRS TEMPTWELL: The right bones this time. I'll laugh when I touch the ashes of thy kind, Mary Traverse.

MARY: I see. (*Pause.*) Perhaps you're right. But you could simply become addicted to counting bodies. And greed can attach itself to anyone. So. (*Pause.*) Let me have the child.

SOPHIE: You can't decide for anyone, Mary.

MARY: The child is mine.

SOPHIE: She's not yours. You gave her birth, that's all. Let her decide, when she's ready, when she knows.

MARY: Give her to me.

SOPHIE: She likes to watch the street.

MRS TEMPTWELL: She'll see men on their way to be hanged at
    Tyburn. That's why we took these lodgings. It's the best
    attended amusement in London.
    (*Over this,* SOPHIE *has begun to sing an incredibly beautiful
    song. She moves away from both of them and goes on singing.*)
MARY: Listen.
MRS TEMPTWELL: Shouts for death.
MARY: Listen to Sophie. Ha. A gracenote there.
    (SOPHIE *sings, watching the street.*)
    What are you looking at, Sophie, what is it you see?
SOPHIE: Look at the stone. The carved stone.
MARY: The new houses. Soft grey lines sloping against the
    London sky.
    (SOPHIE *sings.*)
    Do I have it all wrong? Sing, Sophie. If I were God your
    song would appease me and I would forgive the history of
    the world.
SOPHIE: (*Giving* MARY *the child*) Touch a baby's skin. It's the
    same thing.
MRS TEMPTWELL: There's the cart. See who's in there, Sophie,
    and then sing to us.
SOPHIE: (*Screams*) Jack!

SCENE 2

Tyburn. SOPHIE, MRS TEMPTWELL *and* MARY *holding her baby.
A* MAN *pulls a cart.* JACK *is inside, alone.* LORD EXRAKE *follows
the cart.*

SOPHIE: Jack!
MARY: I thought it would be Lord Gordon.
SOPHIE: Jack!
MRS TEMPTWELL: You don't like to hang lords.
SOPHIE: Jack. Speak to me. Jack.
    (JACK *is silent.*)
MAN: Let the cart pass.

LORD EXRAKE: Is he going to say something?

MARY: Lord Exrake!

LORD EXRAKE: Hello, my dear. Who are you? Forgive me . . .
my memory. What a sweet child. Not mine, I hope. No:
too young. These days . . .

SOPHIE: Jack. It's me. Sophie. Speak to me.
(JACK *is silent*.)

LORD EXRAKE: Sophie . . . means wisdom. I have loved . . .
Did you ask why I'm here? I've found a way to go to sleep.
I listen to what they say before they're hanged. I repeat
their last words and it makes me sleep. Try it.

MARY: Is there no grace, somewhere?

LORD EXRAKE: (*To the* MAN) When will he talk?

MAN: Don't know. Some of them make jokes at the end. Some
tell their lives, give speeches. I've never seen one who
wouldn't talk.

LORD EXRAKE: Silence. Silence at the very end. Would that
make me sleep?

SOPHIE: (*To* MARY) You know he didn't do anything. Tell
them!

MARY: Who will listen?

MRS TEMPTWELL: Sing to her, Sophie.

MAN: (*To* JACK) Look, I know how you feel. Animals out there,
aren't they? But you have a wife, right? Someone, anyway.
Children? Well, there's a way you can take care of them
when you're dead. Nothing magic. I work for this man: all
you have to do is say this word we tell you and we'll look
after your widow and any woman. What about it?

SOPHIE: Jack!

MAN: Look, she's crying for you. You don't want her to go
hungry, do you? All you have to do is say, before the man
– you know. Just before. All you say is: Drink Olvitie. Got
it? Drink Olvitie. That's all.

LORD EXRAKE: That's what a man said a few weeks ago. Drink
Olvitie. I've been drinking it ever since.

MAN: Remember that: drink Olvitie, and she'll be looked
after.

SOPHIE: (*To* MARY) You did all this. You should be up there. Go on. Kill your child. Here, I'll put it under the wheel for you.

MARY: Sophie, no. Not now. Not from you. I know we can . . . we will find.

MRS TEMPTWELL: You won't.

LORD EXRAKE: Have you lost something, my dear? Perhaps I can help you. What won't she find?

MRS TEMPTWELL: Grace. She hasn't the right.

SOPHIE: Jack!

MARY: Come with me, Sophie. We will grieve, but we won't despair. Come.
(MARY *takes* SOPHIE *in her arms and turns away her head.* JACK *stares, impassive. Silence.*)

LORD EXRAKE: Silence. Not even a curse.

Schubert's Adagio in E flat major op. post. 148 'Notturno'

SCENE 3

A garden in the Potteries. MARY, SOPHIE, GILES, LITTLE MARY.

MARY: Beauty. Seen, unseen. I want to touch the light on the river. But we can't even see light. Perhaps one day we'll understand it.

GILES: Are you still trying to understand everything?

SOPHIE: When you told me the world was made up of little particles, Mary, I cried for days.

GILES: I was unhappy when I found out how old the world was.

MARY: I love your wrinkles, father.

GILES: Are there not things it is better not to know? Others it is best to forget?

SOPHIE: No. We must not forget.

MARY: And now the light lifts itself, streaks the chimneys. Gone.

GILES: Where's little Mary? I'll take her in.

(MRS TEMPTWELL *comes on.*)

MRS TEMPTWELL: This is my father's land. Try to throw me off.

GILES: No. That much I have learned. Other things too . . . but I'm old. Speak to them.

MARY: I'm certain that when we understand it all, it'll be simpler, not more confusing. One day we'll know how to love this world.

MRS TEMPTWELL: Will you know how to make it just?

GILES: Mary!

MARY: There she is.

(*Blackout.*)